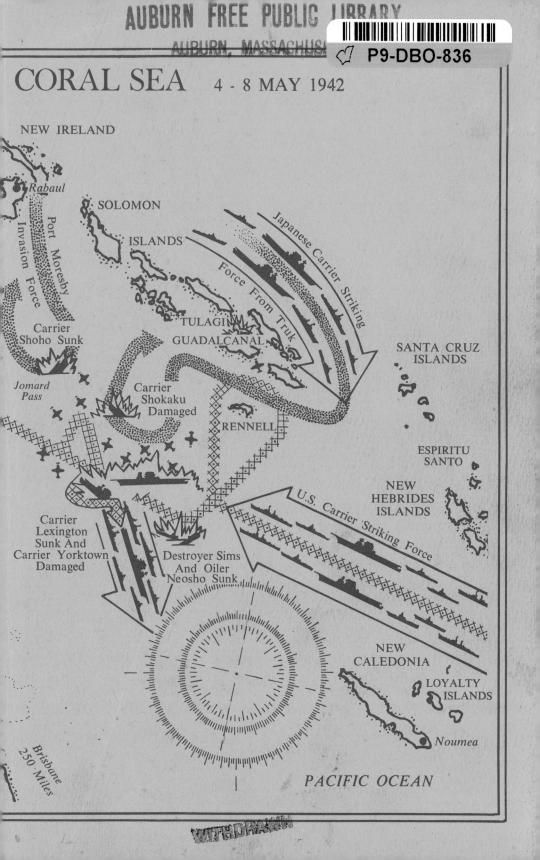

The
LEXINGTON
Goes Down

Also by A. A. Hoehling

THE LAST VOYAGE OF THE LUSITANIA

LAST TRAIN FROM ATLANTA

EMDEN
(*also published as* LONELY COMMAND)

EDITH CAVELL
(*also published as* A WHISPER OF ETERNITY)

THEY SAILED INTO OBLIVION

THE FIERCE LAMBS

THE GREAT EPIDEMIC

WHO DESTROYED THE HINDENBURG?

THE WEEK BEFORE PEARL HARBOR

THE GREAT WAR AT SEA

WOMEN WHO SPIED

THE JEANNETTE EXPEDITION

AMERICA'S ROAD TO WAR, 1939–41

VICKSBURG: 47 DAYS OF SIEGE
(*with the Editors of the
Army Times Publishing Company*)

The
LEXINGTON
Goes Down

A. A. Hoehling

PRENTICE-HALL, Inc.
Englewood Cliffs, New Jersey

The *Lexington* Goes Down by A. A. Hoehling
Copyright © 1971 by A. A. Hoehling
Copyright under International and Pan American
Copyright Conventions
ISBN 0-13-535252-5
Library of Congress Catalog Card Number: 70-130011
Printed in the United States of America   T
Prentice-Hall International, Inc., London
Prentice-Hall of Australia, Pty. Ltd., Sydney
Prentice-Hall of Canada, Ltd., Toronto
Prentice-Hall of India Private Ltd., New Delhi
Prentice-Hall of Japan, Inc., Tokyo

THIS IS THE ACCOUNT OF A FEW HOURS OF
MINGLED GLORY, FEAR AND AGONY OF
A GALLANT LADY, AND ESPECIALLY OF THE
HEROIC CREWMEN WHO SOUGHT TO SAVE
THEIR SHIP, TOLD ALMOST ENTIRELY
IN THEIR OWN WORDS.
TO THEM,
THE LIVING AND THE DEAD,
THIS NARRATIVE IS DEDICATED.

Introduction

The 43,000-ton *Lexington* was the fourth of her name to fly Old Glory. The first, a 16-gun brig, originally the *Wild Duck,* saw duty throughout the Revolution. The second, a 127-foot sloop, sailed the world's oceans to protect United States' commerce as well as the fishing fleets. A large sidewheeler heavily armed, the third, performed yeoman service for the Federal Navy in the Mississippi and Red rivers during the Civil War.

The *Lexington,* CV-2—the nation's second aircraft carrier—had been designed as a 7-funnelled battle cruiser. Work commenced in 1920 at the Bethlehem Shipyard, Fore River, Massachusetts, then was halted the next year by the Washington Limitations of Armaments Conference.

Construction was resumed, however, in 1922. Blueprints were altered to convert the hull and that of a sister into the newest of naval vessels—the "flattop." Even so, too much of World War I vintage marine engineering and materials had crept onto the ways at Fore River. It was as though in some incongruous fashion the heavy formality of a Rembrandt had been embellished by the brush strokes of a modern surrealist.

When commissioned in December, 1927, the *Lexington* became one of the largest men-o'-war afloat. She and her sister, the *Saratoga,* were each 888 feet long, with a 106-foot beam, and drew 24 feet of water. Their flight decks, of splinter-resistant teakwood, extended the lengths of the carriers, with a slight overhang at the bow.

All the superstructure was compressed into a curious, rather flat "island" fore and aft of the single, massive funnel. The bridges, control and communications areas, together with command quarters, were concentrated within this towering

6

"island" on the starboard. Its counterweight was found in the fuel oil tanks on the opposite side.

If her cast-iron mains, for example, were Victorian, the *Lexington*'s propulsion was dramatically of the future: turbo-electric drive. Steam generators supplied electricity for eight huge motors. In turn, these produced 180,000 horsepower, combined, to spin four mammoth bronze propellers. Even to-day, the *Lexington*'s top speed of 35 knots is exceeded only by destroyers and cruisers among the larger vessels of war. She could steam 25 knots in reverse.

Thus, she became one of the fastest, mightiest of war-ships. By the same token, there existed almost everything for the crew's comfort: from ice cream, fresh milk and steaks to nightly movies within the hangar deck. This latter area occupied about two-thirds of the carrier's belowdecks length and was surrounded by compartmented areas of usable space, all of which could be sealed off from the bridge to increase the ship's watertight integrity.

Her aviation gasoline storage served the dual function of reservoir and ballast. The carrier was fitted with fourteen tall columnar tanks, seven on each side of a section of the center line (or keel, a massive longitudinal beam, taller than a man) extending up to about two decks below the hangar, or main deck. Gasoline was moved from these tanks to the planes by pumping seawater into the bottom of the tanks. The fuel floating on top of the heavier water was thereby forced into the lines and hoses, eventually to the planes.

While most of the fo'c'sles, or living quarters, girdling the hangar deck were fitted with fold-back bunks, a small percentage of the crew—the lowest ratings—still took their "sack time" in hammocks: another breath of yesterday.

The *Lexington*'s armament was heavy for a ship designed to be protected by her own aircraft: a main battery of 8-inch rifles in turrets, with a secondary of twelve 5-inch antiaircraft guns and nests of rapid-firing guns of various calibers in tubs and blisters below the flight deck.

The carrier was commissioned on December 14, 1927.

7

Captain Albert Ware Marshall, who had served in the Spanish-American War and helped sow the North Sea mine barrage in 1918, conned the heavyweight down the Fore River in a light snowstorm, almost scraping bottom.

If *"Lady Lex"* quickly gained a reputation as a "happy ship," she did harbor a few less desirable qualities—such as an affinity to roll. This was a natural response in beam seas to her slim waist, a 9–1 ratio of length to width. The carrier's exaggerated turning circle of nearly a mile, at least twice that of a cruiser, demanded nimble seamanship on the part of her escorts.

Based at San Pedro, the *Lexington* was a mother hen to the battle fleet in far-ranging exercises from the Aleutians south to the Canal Zone. Together with the *Saratoga,* she trained many of the pilots who would have squadron responsibility when war "games" would be played in earnest.

Her greyhound speed became legend. Once she steamed from San Pedro to Honolulu, more than 2,200 nautical miles, in but a few minutes more than seventy-two hours. She could have done it even faster.

She also proved that her 140,800-kilowatt electric capacity *was* sufficient for the needs of a large city. In fact, she supplied current for Tacoma, Washington, for three weeks in December, 1929. Low streams had shut down the municipal power plant.

In July, 1937, the *Lexington* was *grande dame* in a large naval force searching for Amelia Earhart. The 39-year-old aviatrix had crash-landed, it was theorized, somewhere in the South Pacific on a round-the-world flight. Howland Island had been her last destination.

While Miss Earhart was never found, Navy pilots were afforded an unusual opportunity to practice open-ocean navigation. The carrier had sailed on such short notice that the complement was soon reduced to eating beans and dehydrated potatoes, and to rolling cigarettes from pipe or chewing tobacco.

It was all a part of the availability and readiness of a very special ship.

CONTENTS

NAVY TIME

Midnight	0000
2 minutes after midnight	0002
12:30 A.M.	0030
1:00 A.M.	0100
2:00 A.M.	0200
and so on until—	
12:00 noon	1200
1:00 P.M.	1300
2:00 P.M.	1400
2:30 P.M.	1430

Thus, the twenty-four hours in the day are counted continuously around the clock, making 11:55 P.M. "2355" by adding twelve hours to the expressed time.

From rock and tempest, fire and foe,
Protect them whereso'er they go;
Thus evermore shall rise to Thee
Glad hymns of praise from land and sea.
　　　　　　—UNITED STATES NAVY HYMN

The *Lexington,* designed as a battle cruiser in 1918, was the product of another era. Youngsters among her crew at the time of Pearl Harbor thought much the same about many of their shipmates, some of whom had been aboard since the carrier was commissioned in 1927. Cecil "Pat" Dowling, in the Navy since World War I, posed beside his Ford touring car, also of "early vintage."

COURTESY OF COMMANDER DOWLING

Commissioned in December, 1927, the *Lexington* was one of the largest men o'war afloat.

BETHLEHEM STEEL COMPANY

NATIONAL ARCHIVES

Medical examinations were part of shipboard routine.

NATIONAL ARCHIVES

"Lady Lex" quickly gained a reputation as a "happy ship," and undoubtedly the ship's glee club enlivened her days at sea.

NATIONAL ARCHIVES

PART 1

A HURT GIANT

1

". . . then HELL broke loose!"

At 1108 on Friday, May 8, 1942, in the Coral Sea, according to the navigator's log, the *Lexington* "changed speed to 25 knots.

"1111, a signal to the force for course 125°, speed 20 knots was executed, but course was not changed by this ship.

"1115, first enemy aircraft seen on port bow."

Flying in the lead, the first enemy plane appeared to a supply officer as "a slick-looking torpedo plane, the first time I guess we've seen the big new torpedo plane the Japs have, and they *really* roared in!"

"1116, gunfire opened on enemy, speed increased to 30 knots. Torpedo planes seen on starboard bow. Rudder was put full left but before ship started to swing left, rudder was again put full right.

"1118, torpedo hit port side about frame 50."

A correspondent on board scribbled: "1118½, the *Lexington* shudders under our feet and a heavy blast spouts mingled flame and water on our port side forward.

"A torpedo explosion and we can see the wakes of others streaking toward us."

The captain, leaning over the conning bridge, would observe, "The water in all directions seemed full of torpedo wakes. Bombs were also dropping all around us."

In sky aft, a gunnery officer turned from his Mark 19 antiaircraft director to see what the young ensign on the outboard director wanted to say to him, even as "an odd glazed look came into his eyes . . . and he fell over."

The ship's air officer mused amidst his streaming radio orders, "Now we're going to get a real Navy yard overhaul."

In the steamy forward pump room, however, ten stories or more below the air officer's eminence, the reaction of Fireman First Class Vernon Highfill would be shared by very many of his shipmates:

". . . then HELL broke loose!"

2

". . . like she was a prima donna."

As war clouds darkened in 1941, the veteran *Lexington* was entering her second year under the command of Captain Frederick Carl Sherman. The carrier's ninth skipper was an accomplished ship handler and a disciple of all that the term "taut" implied.

"Ted"—so named since boyhood to differentiate him from his father, known as "Fred"—awed junior officers by his ability to dock the huge vessel without tugs, if necessary. Staffers were not expected to be quite *that* dexterous, but they must be "Navy."

The short, stocky native of Port Huron, Michigan, graduated twentieth in a class of 130 from the United States Naval Academy in 1910. He won his *N* in lacrosse and further honors as a boxer. For World War I service as commander of the submarine 0-7, Sherman received the Navy Cross.

The Navy was not only Sherman's life, it was him. While a most capable officer, he was nonetheless not especially prepossessing. He wore glasses much of the time and chain-smoked, using a black holder containing another cigarette as a filter. Ashes frequently flecked the lapels of his uniform. A sweet tooth could be blamed for a certain pudginess.

His toughness rating was second only to that of a previous commander of the *Lexington,* Admiral Ernest J. King. Discipline was Frederick Sherman's credo, a source of strength and inspiration. Some avowed his stern presence spawned a loneliness inside of him, evident even at the bridge table where he was also master.

Sherman knew how to dress down a subordinate for what was purported inefficiency or ignorance of regulations. Once he summarily ordered a junior officer off the ship for authorizing the turning of a propeller at anchor. Unfortunately the big blade slammed into a battle raft moored alongside.

The captain detached another hapless ensign simply because he did not consider him sufficiently "Navy." The officer was supposedly lax in his duties.

On the other hand, the captain sometimes was forced by circumstances to issue orders hardly covered in that bible of the Annapolis-oriented, *The Watch Officers Guide.* Once his cocker spaniel, Wags, raced so fast across the deck that he tumbled into the water. "Man overboard!" was sounded. A boat was lowered "on the double" to recover the ten-year-old pet.

"Admiral Wags" literally was top dog on this ship. He slept beneath his master's bunk, under the chart table or wherever fancy teased. Long ago, Wags had developed a taste for rich, frosted cake. Nothing was denied this cocker, a canine that perforce remained a nightmare for the "swabbies," the young seaman who had to keep the decks mopped and clean.

In likelihood, too few knew the humbler side of Captain Sherman. Once he administered a sharp dressing down to a petty officer who—seemingly, of all curious errors!—had saluted him first. It turned out that the noncommissioned officer was wearing the Medal of Honor.

22

Traditionally, in all of the military services, the wearer of the nation's highest award must himself first be saluted, even if it is a case—unlikely enough—of a five-star admiral saluting a seaman second class.

There were ever-increasing hints these last, tired weeks of 1941 that the United States, as President Franklin Roosevelt had forecast, would soon be experiencing her rendezvous with destiny.

Previously installed on the *Lexington* was a top-secret device known as "radar," perfected at about the same time by the British and Americans. The United States Army Signal Corps had successfully tested such an ultrasonic-wave set in 1937. The *Lexington's* Model CXAM, one of but half a dozen thus far provided by the Navy, was indication enough that the fleet must be on guard against perils unseen.

When eighteen Marine-piloted scout planes for Midway Island were loaded aboard the carrier, there seemed further certainty that danger lay across the Pacific.

Although it may have seemed that the high command in Washington slept through the final, fateful weeks of 1941, war *was* in the air. Its possibility was sufficiently in the forefront of the mind of Lieutenant (jg.) Asbury "Red" Coward, from Wynwood, Pennsylvania, to cause him to inquire of an engineering inspector just how many torpedoes he believed the *Lexington* could sustain. The answer: "about twelve."

It sounded reassuring enough to "Red," who had been aboard ever since his graduation from the Naval Academy in 1938. He was in command of "sky aft," consisting of a battery of 5-inch, 20-mm. guns just behind the stack. Like "sky forward," this was an antiaircraft position.

On Friday, December 5, the *Lexington* put Ford Island astern as she departed Honolulu for Midway, 1,200 miles northwest of Hawaii and 2,800 miles east of Japan. The carrier operated under war conditions, although the nation was still "at peace." She zigzagged day and night, guns manned, lower deck hatches battened.

23

The *West Virginia* and the *Tennessee* burn fiercely at Pearl Harbor,
December 7, 1941. U.S. NAVY PHOTOGRAPH

Captain Frederick Carl Sherman.

Captain Sherman and "Admiral Wags."

COURTESY OF MRS. FREDERICK SHERMAN

Chaplain George Laclede Markle.

U.S. NAVY PHOTOGRAPH

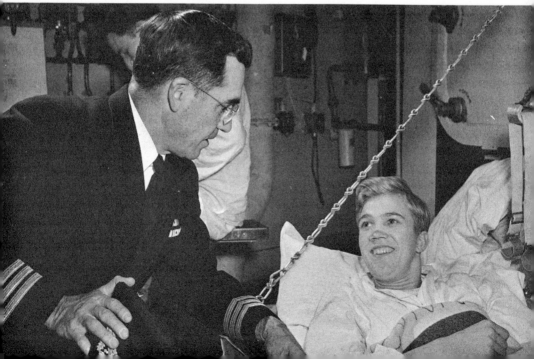

On Saturday a multiengined monoplane was sighted. The time was about 1400 hours. The stranger vanished over the horizon without being identified.

On Sunday, December 7, the carrier was 400 miles southeast of Midway, approaching launch point for her Marine pilots, when the radioman took an incoming message: "Air attack on Pearl. This is no drill." However, in the excitement of the moment, the letters of the last word were typed "dripp." In spite of the overwhelming gravity, the officers obtained a momentary chuckle.

The amusement quickly subsided. Commander James R. Dudley, from Hannibal, Missouri, a 1921 graduate of Annapolis, the navigation officer and also an aviator, handed the "thing" to Sherman. Authenticity was never questioned, and the news was at once passed through loudspeakers to all hands aboard:

"Now hear this . . . !"

The customary stentorian preface of a bos'n was followed by the softer tones of the chaplain, Commander George Laclede Markle. The 56-year-old Presbyterian minister from New Castle, Pennsylvania, then became the *Lexington*'s newscaster.

Although badly needed on Midway, the Marine planes were hurriedly "struck" (transferred) below to the hangar deck. The recall was especially frustrating to the pilots. Fred Hartson, a young aviation machinist mate 2d from Portsmouth, New Hampshire, had been impressed by the devil-may-care twist at the moustache of one of the Marines as he waited beside his scout plane. Something of the *éclat* from World War I. . . .

"Our mission was immediately changed," wrote Lieutenant J. F. Roach, assistant medical officer on the carrier. "We headed in a southerly direction, apparently with the purpose of locating the Japanese and carrying out an attack on their force."

The *Lexington* was aiming at a rendezvous with the *Enterprise*. Aboard the latter carrier was the peppery Rear Ad-

27

miral William F. "Bull" Halsey. It was he who had framed the message to "intercept and destroy" the enemy force of carriers, battleships, cruisers and other escorts that must have mounted the attack on Pearl Harbor.

It did not matter that he had no valid information on *where* this hostile fleet was.

When the soft-spoken navigator, Jim Dudley, observed that Halsey's order was "one hell of a big assignment," Captain Sherman laconically replied, "But look at the target!"

That same Sunday, about 1300 hours, a small tramp steamer was sighted on a westerly course. While there was speculation that this might have been a mother ship for one-man submarines, the *Lexington* had no time to investigate.

"After several days of unsuccessful searching south of Oahu," wrote Dudley, "we entered Pearl to refuel and reprovision."

In the confusion of the days, the *Lexington's* fleet tanker had lost her hose couplings when a cruiser, "filling up," raced off after a (false) submarine contact. Simultaneously another cruiser, the *Portland,* hunting for a lost pilot who had bailed out, was bombed by a PBY patrol plane whose pilot thought she was a Japanese carrier and her escorting destroyer an enemy cruiser.

Although the PBY's aim was fortunately poor, the aircraft itself was almost shot down by *Lexington* fighters. They had been alerted for an "enemy air raid."

It was no wonder, as Dr. Roach himself postscripted, that most on board were "in a quite disappointed state." The frame of mind in Hawaii was worse yet. Dudley was impressed by the greeting from a launch coming alongside the newly arrived carrier: "Thank God. It's nice to see a ship that's afloat."

Wreckage lay everywhere. The blackened mast alone attested to where the *Arizona,* once among the largest battleships in the world, had been moored. Vessels such as the

Oklahoma, lying on beam ends on the harbor bottom, looked like oversize beached whales.

The *Lexington,* however, did not have much time to fill up and steam out again.

"We headed southwest to the far Pacific," Dr. Roach continued in his own diary, "with the hope of finding some Japanese forces or some Japanese base that we might attack."

The carrier's operations were not quite so haphazard, however. She was under orders to bomb Jaluit in the Marshalls. Very shortly she was diverted toward a sister atoll, Wotje, and finally brought home without having drawn blood.

Quickly she put Diamond Head astern once more, now navigating towards Bougainville Island, in the Solomons, with the intent of making an attack on the Japanese base at Rabaul, New Britain Island, in the Bismarck Archipelago.

". . . The day before the scheduled attack, our planes scouted thoroughly," wrote Dr. Roach, "and found no sight of the enemy. The following morning [February 20] we continued to head in, hoping to be at the outer limit of the Japanese scouting screen at about noontime.

"At approximately 11 o'clock, a Japanese snooper was sighted, flying one of the large Japanese flying boats of the type they call Kawanishi. The snooper was immediately attacked by our fighters and shot down. However, he apparently had time to make his contact report before he was destroyed. It was then I realized that the surprise element of our attack had been compromised. Therefore, we changed plans and headed south.

"Along about 4 o'clock, we expected there might be an attack on us by land-based aircraft. And at the appointed time the Japanese planes appeared. They approached in two waves. The first I believe contained 11 planes. These were two-motored land bombers."

Lieutenant Thomas Jones Nixon III, a slender, dark-haired North Carolinian and Annapolis graduate, '37, was experiencing his first combat. He was in 8-inch control aft

29

(directing the two stern turrets for the big 8-inch guns), "a good point from which to watch the entire show." He reported:

"We had worked out a doctrine for using the main battery against low-flying torpedo planes by shooting into the ocean and throwing up a splash of water in their path of approach. I had also armed my men in the control station with .30 caliber rifles to use against dive bombers. But this was with the hope of keeping them occupied rather than with any faith in this defense. These Jap planes approaching were, however, horizontal bombers against which we could do nothing but watch and hope.

". . . My reaction was entirely interest, all-absorbing and fascinating to the almost complete exclusion of any other reaction. I felt little fear, foolishly enough, after the enemy planes came into view, only while waiting in the control station listening to the loudspeaker reports on their approach.

"I distinctly remember the exultation as I saw the Jap bombers falling into the sea, one of which fell fairly close to the ship and exploded as it hit, forming a mass of flames over the water.

"I felt matter-of-factly about the crew of that bomber—just a few more Japs gone to join their ancestors. Later, I was a bit remorseful about this reaction. Those Japs probably all had families back in Nippon.

"Did they really feel as happy to die for their emperor as the newspapers would have us believe?"

Of the eighteen enemy planes that had attacked the *Lexington,* only one was known positively to have made good its escape. During this first major United States carrier action, a stocky, quiet naval aviator from Chicago made air history. Lieutenant Edward H. "Butch" O'Hare alone and in a few minutes shot down five enemy planes.*

An air-to-surface encounter, however dramatic and, to some, frightening, meant different things to different combatants. It all depended on one's battle station and duty.

---

*O'Hare wore his Medal of Honor but a few months. He was lost on a mission when his wingman fired in error.

"The injury to personnel which we received aboard," observed Dr. Roach, "amounted to just a few scratches and minor wounds from shrapnel and one case of bullet wound from a Japanese machine gun. . . . An interesting sidelight on this engagement was the fact that an appendectomy was necessarily performed during the attack."

The *Lexington* had challenged the Japanese menace to the southwest Pacific and especially the supply routes to Tokyo's newly seized base at Rabaul, 300 miles west of Bougainville.

Already more than 3,500 miles from Hawaii, the carrier steamed even farther away from home port as she swept into the Coral Sea, a halcyon waterway of Melanesia, sheltered by the Great Barrier Reef to the west, the Solomons to the north, the New Hebrides and New Caledonia to the east and southeast.

In the nearby Gulf of Papua, New Guinea, on March 10, the carrier's aircraft, heavy with gasoline and bombs, waddled upward for altitude like obese pelicans, barely above the shimmering blue waters. Ultimately they struggled over the three-mile-high Owen-Stanley Mountains of southern New Guinea, barely clearing passes through austere peaks to catch the enemy off guard in the harbors of Lae and Salamaua. These two gold-field ports in the Huon Gulf had become Japanese assembly areas.

Not an American plane was lost in the raid on Lae and Salamaua. In their wake, the pilots, some of whom had once searched these waters for Amelia Earhart, had left a number of transports, destroyers and small escorts in flames.

The foe's grand strategy to seize Port Moresby on the southwest coast of New Guinea was disrupted. In fact, during subsequent abortive attempts to capture the port through an overland trek, the soldiers of Emperor Hirohito were lost by the thousands to disease and starvation in the jungles.

The *Lexington* now was "something," even more so than she had always been, both to those who called her home and the families who would watch for the first glimpse of the distinctive silhouette hauling in past Point Loma Light, at the entrance to San Diego Bay. Commander Edward Beck, Class of 1925, commanding the large destroyer *Phelps,* expressed the opinion of many when he observed of the carrier: "We had followed her many thousands of miles and had learned to look upon her as a symbol of invincibility. It was always a comfort to be in company with her and her air groups."

The feeling worked both ways. The destroyers and whatever cruisers, such as the *Portland,* could be scraped up in the war's desperate early months protected *Lady Lex,* as one crewman put it, "like she was a prima donna."

She had become indispensable in 1942's species of naval war. However, she also needed some face-lifting. For one thing, the Navy Department had become convinced of "the uselessness of turret guns on aircraft carriers." They also tended to make the ships somewhat top-heavy.

The *Lexington,* therefore, was ordered back to Pearl for the removal of hundreds of tons of excess "fat" represented by the four turrets and their dual mounts of the 8-inch guns, which could not elevate onto attacking aircraft. They could only cause a big splash of water on the off chance of damaging or distracting torpedo planes roaring in at a low level.

Some of the complement was detached. New officers and men were put aboard, making a total of 2,951 including pilots and a few civilian technicians or observers, plus one correspondent. This was the largest number ever accommodated on the *Lexington,* with a designed capacity of approximately 2,200.

Among those reporting aboard was Lieutenant (jg.) Max Price, of Charleston, West Virginia. "Maxy" was not only an athlete and a good student but, as well, known by his shipmates as the best looking member of the Class of 1939.

The carrier would head back to sea with eighteen fighters, thirty-six dive-bombers and twelve torpedo planes, for an air group of sixty-six planes, which, in turn, composed four squadrons. They were under the command of a veteran pilot, Commander William Bowen "Bill" Ault, an Oregonian and star on the Academy basketball team prior to graduation in 1922.

"This refit period also gave me a chance to see my wife occasionally," Nixon said, in voicing the sentiments of many, "a rare privilege for a *Lexington* officer after December 7."

During this brief refuge from the war, Vice Admiral Wilson Brown, a 60-year-old Philadelphian who had been in command of *Lexington* Task Force 11, was relieved by Rear Admiral Aubrey Wray Fitch. Brown's health had failed to the extent that he was unable to move up and down ladders without assistance.

"Jake" Fitch, of St. Ignace, Michigan, Class of '06, but one year Brown's junior, was one of the shortest of his rank in the Navy. Fit, efficient and endowed with humor and understanding, he possessed a sentimental attachment for the *Lex*. He had watched a portion of her fitting out in the 1920's and commanded her in 1936.

On April 15, Air Task Force 11 put back to sea. Its nucleus, the *Lexington,* was one of but five American carriers throughout the expanse of the Pacific, from the Auckland Islands to the Aleutians.

3

"Scratch one flattop!"

Rumors engulfed the living spaces of the *Lexington*. The formidable Japanese bases on Truk and Rabaul would be the next targets. The former, 800 miles north of New Britain, was easily among the most heavily defended Japanese holdings in the Pacific.

Some few also believed Truk, 2,400 miles west of Howland Island, was the secret reconnaissance object of Miss Earhart's ill-fated flight. In early 1942, however, Truk was out of a small task force's class. In these uncertain waters it was challenge enough to mount daily ASW (antisubmarine) air patrols.

Wary, ever probing for the enemy, the *Lexington* was—or so Captain Sherman hoped—a taut ship, but not necessarily a tense one. Life, punctuated with little diversions, went on. Some nights there were movies within the auditorium-like hangar deck. When it was blacked out and the huge plane elevators were down, there were two patches of blue, starry sky, as though one were in an observatory.

Off duty, officers and enlisted personnel alike, could, as always, indulge their hobbies. Those manually-adapted turned to the lathes in the carpenter shop to fashion souvenirs for their families. Tom Nixon, for one, was hard at work on a wooden bread tray.

There were also the little chores to perform in answer to the whims associated with command. The "old man" on the *Lexington,* for example, had to be supplied with "spaghetti" for his spectacles. This was simply insulation, as over electrical wires, to keep Sherman's temple pieces from chafing in the constant sweaty temperatures.

The atmosphere in the wardroom was relaxed under the beneficent reign of the new executive officer, Commander Morton Seligman, a stocky extravert from Santa Fe, New Mexico. "Mort," who was with the Class of '19, presided over the officers' dining area, as was the prerogative of "execs." Smooth-faced and pleasant, Seligman, for some whim, had toted along his golf clubs and fishing tackle.

With a few exceptions, the junior officers and warrants dined separately in their own rooms. One such exception was Ensign Harold E. "Willie" Williamson of Brockton, Massachusetts, a 1940 graduate of Annapolis. Wardroom privileges were extended to him since he was an electrical division officer.

When the carrier crossed the Equator, war was put briefly aside for traditional "line" ceremonies. Commander Walter Gilmore, gray and jowly, became Grand Inquisitor above the pollywogs.

A Navy supply officer in Brest during World War I, Gilmore had long been legendary for the adequacy of his sea stores, even to little things such as toothpicks and napkin racks. The *Lexington*'s chief supply officer, however, had put on far too much weight over the years. He could descend conventional ship's iron ladders—some vertical, most nearly so—only with consummate difficulty. His poundage, however, was no factor in Gilmore's popularity. He was a favorite throughout the carrier.

This period, en route to the enemy, tended to foster an illusion of invincibility. The belief was strengthened, as one officer phrased it, that we could "take on any four Jap carriers."

Off the Australian coast, west of the New Hebrides, a few of the *Lexington's* planes flew overnight into Townsville. The pilots returned with bottles of Scotch, the first liquor seen by at least the junior officers on board a naval vessel, together with interesting stories about their evening ashore.

In the meanwhile, on broader canvas, the "war in the Pacific," as Captain Sherman observed, "had not been going well for the democracies." This was a creditable example of understatement.

President Roosevelt was pronouncing the whole outlook "very grave." Prime Minister Churchill, over his brandy glass, was conceding the possibility of a hitherto unthinkable: negotiated peace.

Singapore, "Gibraltar of the East," surrendered on February 15, 1942. Great Britain, the United States and the Netherlands lost an entire squadron (including Roosevelt's favorite cruiser, the *Houston*) the end of the same month in the unbelievable Battle of the Java Sea.

Bataan fell on April 9. Corregidor Island, at the entrance to Manila harbor, was going. General Joseph W. "Vinegar Joe" Stillwell, retreating from Burma, admitted to "a terrible licking." None could charge it was of his own doing.

Lieutenant Colonel James H. Doolittle's flight of sixteen B-25 medium bombers from the deck of the carrier *Hornet* on April 18 to bomb Tokyo, Nagoya and Kobe provided a boost to a nation whose morale was in the doldrums. The surprise raid, however, was of no military value and did not slow the flood tide of conquest by one minute. However, it *did* inspire the foe to augment the naval defenses of his home waters.

On May 1 the *Lexington* steamed into the Coral Sea to join Rear Admiral Frank Jack Fletcher's Task Force 17. This was composed of the newer carrier *Yorktown,* which had been so busy since December 7 that she already was known as the "Waltzing Matilda." Fletcher, an Iowan and classmate of Fitch's, became tactical commander of this largest sea-air striking assemblage yet mustered by the United States. It included as well His Majesty's Australian cruisers *Australia* and *Hobart* which, with the U.S.S. *Chicago,* a heavy cruiser, operated under the command of Rear Admiral J. G. Crace, Royal Navy.

American intelligence, which had snooped on the Japanese naval as well as diplomatic codes for more than a year, knew that formidable invasion-bent convoys were churning the Coral Sea. The Solomons, New Guinea and Australia herself were apparent objectives.

On May 3 the Imperial Fourth Fleet seized Tulagi, on Florida Island, the principal port and seat of government of the Lower Solomons. The British protectorate was situated only twenty-five miles east of Guadalcanal. Another fleet hauled out of Rabaul, apparently aiming for Port Moresby even as Admiral Isoroku Yamamoto, commander of the Japanese Navy and architect of the Pearl Harbor strike, moved a glowering force into the eastern reaches of the Coral Sea.

Designed to checkmate the American units, the Japanese force was composed of the veteran carriers of December 7: *Shokaku* ("Soaring Crane") and *Zuikaku* ("Happy Crane") both 20,000 tons. They were supported by the lighter *Shoho,* nine cruisers and nearly a dozen destroyers.

On Monday, May 4, aircraft from Fletcher's *Yorktown* swept upward to attack enemy ships in Tulagi. At one time the task force was less than 100 miles offshore. Results were disappointing, although the raid and reconnaissance established that the Japanese had dug in, termite-like, throughout the Solomons.

The bombings and strafings by the Navy planes also inspired Admiral Takeo Takagi to hurl southward at flank speed a task force of two carriers, two heavy cruisers and six destroyers. Takagi, victor in February's Allied disaster in the Java Sea, was convinced that the United States Navy must be present in numbers not in any way predicted by his own intelligence officers.

On the morning of May 5 the big new fleet oiler, *Neosho,* which had steamed out of Pearl Harbor during the height of the attack, arrived to deliver fuel to the task force. The *Lexington* alone carried two million gallons (6,000 tons) of oil to keep her turbines running. This was in addition to aviation gasoline.

The *Neosho* also sent mail aboard. In turn, she received bulging sacks containing official correspondence—requisitions, requests for yard work, nonpriority reports on action at sea—and unofficial mail, as well. These last were the letters home.

Riding high at dusk, the *Neosho,* accompanied by the destroyer *Sims,* hauled off to the southwest. The tanker, appreciably shorter than the *Lexington,* nevertheless was silhouetted on the horizon for a rather long time until finally she was swallowed in the Pacific's immensity.

"On the morning of May 6," Dr. Roach wrote, "our scouts had picked up information that there was a large Japanese force coming down from the north."

Later it was logged in the carrier's air operations, "during the afternoon of May 6 orders were received from Comtaskforce 17 to prepare for air attack upon the enemy forces reported to be concentrated in the vicinity of Misima Island."

On Corregidor Island, nearly 3,000 miles to the northwest, General Jonathan "Skinny" Wainwright was surrendering his sick and starving garrison in abject humiliation, while planes from the two carriers prepared for this morning's attack.

The task force swept through the hot, calm Wednesday night until soundings from picket destroyers warned of the shallows of mountainous, wooded Misima. The carrier herself, steaming usually at 27 knots, remained well offshore, providing "sea room" for launching planes.

Misima was the northernmost of the eighty islands of the Louisiade Archipelago, 120 miles due east of South Cape, New Guinea, and some 400 miles east of the Great Barrier Reef.

At dawn, in a choppy sea under a 17-knot wind, a few

The carrier *Shoho* tries vainly to avoid the bombs and torpedoes from the *Lexington's* and the *Yorktown's* planes.

The *Shoho* is sunk. She was the first enemy carrier casualty of the war in the Pacific.   NATIONAL ARCHIVES

miles south of Rossel Island, one of the Louisiades planes was launched. The radio cry of "Bandits!" almost as soon as the first wave of scouts became airborne announced the presence of the already familiar four-engined Kawanishi reconnaissance aircraft.

Then a spiraling plume of smoke to starboard indicated the death plunge of the lumbering Kawanishi, winged by a Navy fighter. There was a glare of fire, then more smoke as the big craft smacked into the water.

Through a clearing in the overcast, the *Yorktown*'s patrol located the enemy 170 miles northwest. They were joined in minutes by attack aircraft from the *Lex* and, as Captain Sherman phrased it, went into bombing dives "with clocklike precision."

Although the pilots did not know her identity, they soon scored on the *Shoho,* which was "observed to burn fiercely in a manner obviously beyond control." Several severe explosions, other than those resulting from bomb or torpedo hits, were observed, and before the attack was completed, the ship was almost entirely hidden by smoke and flames. Her benediction, of sorts, was pronounced by one of the pilots over the radio crisscross: "What a mess!"

The *Shoho* sank less than fifteen minutes later as the pilots "bent" their throttles to fly home to the carriers in the shortest possible time. There never seemed any reserve supply of gasoline on the anticlimactic return leg of a mission.

Lieutenant Commander Robert E. "Bob" Dixon, a Georgian fifteen years out of Annapolis and a squadron leader, advised the air department of the *Lexington:*

"Scratch one flattop!"

The *Shoho* became the first Japanese carrier sunk in the war. The American Navy had lost three pilots. It turned out that one, however, had crashed-landed on Rossel Island, in the Louisiades. Rescued by friendly natives and a missionary, Ensign A. J. "Tony" Quigley ultimately returned to the war and flying.

The results of this engagement, Dr. Roach would laconically observe, were "very satisfactory." Commander Beck, on the destroyer *Phelps,* thought much the same: "It was our day with the Japs."

Not so satisfactory, however, was a message picked up this Thursday afternoon from the *Neosho,* which so recently had steamed off from the task force. At 1555 she radioed: "Sinking."

Planes from the *Zuikaku* and *Shokaku* had pounced on the fleet auxiliary oiler and her escort, the *Sims,* after the two had erroneously been identified by an enemy scout plane as "carrier and destroyer" instead of tanker and destroyer. The American carriers had been spared from attack by intermittent rain squalls beating down during most of the day.

Although the *Sims* was torn in half by the bombs, the number 2 gun was still being worked without pause, in the great traditions of the service, when both sections of the destroyer plunged under. The empty tanker, aflame, nonetheless remained afloat. Another destroyer, rescuing survivors the next day, sank the derelict with torpedoes.

Aboard the *Russell,* her captain, Lieutenant Commander G. Roy Hartwig, a Detroiter, Class of '24, was especially sobered by the loss. He had been relieved two nights before from the *Neosho* escort on account of a broken fuel-feed pump. The affable Hartwig reflected with mingled bitterness and relief, "Thank God a new destroyer can't be named for *me.*"

(Hartwig's hunch was borne out two years later when the USS *Hyman* slid down the ways at Bath, Maine. She was christened in honor of the late William M. "Buster" Hyman, classmate of Hartwig's who had commanded the *Sims.* The *Hyman* was some 700 tons larger than the *Sims,* sister of the luckier *Russell.*)

4

Twilight

To Commander Arnold E. True of the destroyer *Hammann,* a "feeling of tension in the air" was apparent this late Thursday afternoon. The wind had died down. It was humid, murky, 97°.

The whole ship "sweated like a man in a Turkish bath," it seemed to Stanley Johnston, the reporter for the Chicago *Tribune,* largely enjoying his first war cruise. "Beads of moisture combined to form rivulets which forever coursed down floors, walls and roofs, the bulkheads, decks and sideplates."

The smell of paint, oil and bilges was almost overpowering.

Scouts, which had already reported "ships everywhere," were still aloft, sniffing for other Kawanishi as well as carrier-based enemy aircraft. They had been persistent shadowers of the task force.

From the *Russell's* bridge, Roy Hartwig watched what appeared to be eight latecomers making their final turns off his port beam for the *Yorktown,* or possibly the *Lex.*

"Our boys," he thought. "Thank God they're back!"

Then he noticed that these aircraft were fitted with fixed landing gear in contrast to the American retractable. Some appeared to be twin-engined, a possibility that caused one destroyer to blink toward the *Lexington,* "Do we have any twin-engined planes airborne?"

Aboard the *Morris,* a destroyer squadron flagship, Lieutenant Commander Harry "Beany" Jarrett, Class of '22, decided the drone was different. Nor did the "planform" silhouetted against the sky look right.

"They appeared to want to land," Lieutenant F. F. "Red" Gill, the fighter director officer of the *Lexington,* logged at six minutes past 7 P.M. ("Red" had been a football star at the University of California.) "They flashed on their running lights."

At the same time, with their Aldis or similar signal lights, the planes flashed various letters in the Morse code, and one made the parenthesis sign.

A landing controller on the flight deck of the *Yorktown* positioned his illuminated wand at the *r* position, signifying "you are correct in your approach."

One seaman aboard the *Lexington* was likening the visitors with curious objectivity to "a flight of tired birds coming home to roost." He mused further, "The ocean must be crowded with aircraft carriers."

The first of the planes was very close to completing its landing when it became apparent that none of the pilots knew the day's countersign or the United States Navy lost plane procedure involving the use of the pilot's last name. Keen-eyed American pilots were aware also that the red and green running lights were of "markedly different shade" than the counterparts with which they were familiar.

A destroyer opened fire, then another, followed by the throaty bark of the heavy cruiser *Minneapolis'* guns. The *Lexington*'s gunners were ordered not to shoot.

The descending planes, which must already have been alerted by the unfamiliar wand signals on the flight deck, winked out their running lights and disappeared, as Captain Sherman observed, "into the darkness like a flock of birds flushed by hunters."

At the same time the *Lexington's* commanding officer was concerned that vessels of the task force were shooting, as he thought, "indiscriminately."

The carrier's radar followed the confused intruders for thirty miles eastward, then each "blip" orbited from the bright electronic screens and vanished. This seemed sufficient evidence that the Japanese carriers were no more than an hour's steaming in that direction.

Now arose the obvious possibility of a night surface attack in the hopes of catching the enemy off guard. Perhaps the torpedo planes would take part. Admiral Fletcher, however, quickly resolved upon a course change to the south to avoid "a chance contact during the hours of darkness."

The enemy, of similar mind, wheeled and pounded northward through the still, inky night.

All in all, to Lieutenant Commander Herbert S. Duckworth, from Cape Girardeau, Missouri, the air officer, the evening's performance had been "one of the damnedest things" he had ever witnessed. "Ducky" Duckworth, trim, with close-cropped black hair, had become one of the Navy's early aviators upon graduation from Annapolis with the Class of 1922.

The eventful day of May 7 was over, as much so as a day can truly and finally be ended at sea in wartime. The last screech of an airplane's tires, snubbed by arresting wires, had already echoed into silence, the last dying propeller whine was forgotten and the red-purple stabbings of exhaust had burned out their defiance of late twilight's murk.

Now visible were only the shielded rows of landing lanterns, rimming the deck like footlights of a theater.

However, Sherman, not pleased at the night's passive operation, was yet more annoyed when he learned that Commander Dudley, the navigator, had upped the *Lexington* to full speed.

47

"Back to standard, Mr. Dudley!" the captain barked.

Then, as Jim Dudley would recall, he received a dressing down from Sherman in the latter's emergency cabin, on the bridge, such as he had never experienced in twenty-one years of active duty.

While the great carrier, almost like a living, palpable creature, settled down for the few remaining hours of darkness, men headed for watch yawned, about to taste their coffee and midnight "chow." Others were in their bunks or already asleep.

For the pilots, all quartered forward in "officers country," it would be an especially short night. They were now informed of "going to attack a Japanese force consisting mostly of carriers and escorting cruisers as soon as we could pick them up in the morning."

Tom Nixon would recall that those who "turned in" did so "with the full expectation of a battle the next day. We knew the approximate location of the enemy and thought he knew ours."

Nonetheless, Tom went "peacefully to sleep, feeling ready and prepared for what was to come."

Chaplain Howell Forgy, the handsome, dark-haired former pastor of the First Presbyterian Church in Murray, Kentucky, felt pretty much the same way aboard the escorting *New Orleans*.

"A sober yet confident tension hung over the ship as we climbed into our bunks," noted Forgy, 34-year-old graduate of Princeton Seminary. He was already somewhat of a legend for his encouragement during the Pearl Harbor attack: "Praise the Lord, and pass the ammunition!"

The heavy cruiser, of 9,950 tons, familiar to her crew as *"No-Boat,"* had been among the first to mount a concerted antiaircraft fire at the Japanese planes sweeping over Diamond Head that December 7. Forgy, however, emphasized that as a man of the cloth he could exhort and even cheer but not actually serve the guns.

Another chaplain, Commander Markle, who had informed the *Lexington*'s crew of the Pearl Harbor attack,

48

believed that the morning would bring with it a "red letter day." The bespectacled Markle, in some respects an older version of Forgy, had been in the Navy for sixteen years following World War I service as a Marine.

Inside the noisy, gasoline-smelling hangar deck, Len Olliff, an aviation machinist mate from Statesboro, Georgia, faced a long and rough night's work. There was a bad fuel pump on his SBD "Dauntless" bomber, attached to Squadron VB-2. The lanky, eight-year veteran of the service doubted that he would be able to "knock off" until morning.

There were, however, less than half a dozen "dead heads" below. These were planes that could not be repaired hurriedly on the flight deck because they required special tools. Sometimes, waiting their turn, they were kept overhead, out of the way, on hooks.

Nearby, another aviation machinist, Fred Hartson, from Portsmouth, New Hampshire, was tearing off the ever-stubborn cowling of his TBD "Avenger" torpedo bomber after "they had pulled a 30-hour check on the Pratt and Whitney engines."

It meant cleaning the entire power plant—radial and "fussy" like the rest of them—with carbon tetrachloride. This was not only a reeking job but a dangerous one as well, since the chemical contained poisonous properties. Especially toxic to the liver, it was absorbed readily by sweating pores.

Fred, who had enlisted in the Navy two years previously, took special pride in his plane. For example, he had covered the worn and cracked leather headrest with varicolored cloth found in one of the many mechanics' ragbags dotting the hangar deck. Now the headrest resembled sort of an airborne crazy quilt.

In the chartroom of the *Russell*, dipping pleasantly in the night swell, Hartwig was writing orders under the pale red glow of a single lamp: "Cannot over-estimate the need for constant vigilance. . . ."

Standing the first watch of the new day, May 8, on the *Lexington* was Ensign W. J. "Bill" Keating, '40, of Baltimore. Wary as always not to step on "Wags," who often

49

slept under the chart table, Bill commenced Friday's log with the affirmation, routine now for the past five months: "00-04, engaged in hostilities with Germany, Japan and Italy."

Through the pen of his quartermaster he continued: "Steaming in company with Task Force 17 in special cruising disposition "L", course 150° [southeast], fleet speed 20 knots, 169 RPM's . . . ship darkened and in condition of readiness with material condition of readiness 'Y' set on and below the second deck except for ventilation fittings."

Seven minutes later: "0011, changed fleet course to 180° T and fleet speed to 14 knots (121 RPM). 0116, changed fleet course to 270° T [due west]. 0121, commenced zigzagging according to standard plan. . . ."

On the *Russell*, sweeping faster at a distance abeam, Hartwig continued: ". . . 22 knot speed . . . commenced zigzagging."

The minutes turned into hours this early morning in the Coral Sea.

5

"Break out the sandwiches."

"Maxy" Price took the 4–8 A.M. watch.

The day's activity was now beginning as onyx skies of the short tropical night paled. The familiar reverberating horns announced the ascent of the huge plane elevators.

The duty's officer's log continued in the special vocabulary and grammar of navigation: ". . . 0530, went to flight quarters, 0552 went to general quarters. 0614, turned into the wind and launched morning search. Went ahead standard, 14 knots."

Commander Duckworth sent scouts aloft to comb 270° of the surrounding skies and waters, only one-quarter less than a full circumference. They were accompanied by four fighters. As usual, torpedo and dive bombers warmed up on deck for word of a possible target within the maximum scouting range of 200 miles.

"Completed launching about 0635."

Twelve fully armed torpedo bombers remained in readiness, their propellers turning.

Len Olliff had almost finished with his cranky fuel pump. He figured on a shower and "some shuteye" in his compartment on the port side forward. Like other living spaces, this one doubled as dormitory and mess hall.

After the shower, clean skivvies and the rest of "fatigue" dress, tropical modification. For the working mechanics, this could and usually did mean frayed blue jeans.

Fred Hartson's plane got off. He was scrubbing up his area of the hangar deck. The slight, meticulous Fred was worried about the "mess" throughout the yawning area.

It was, as most, a quiet general quarters. For the sensitive —those who could not satisfactorily rationalize the possibility of being sunk and maybe drowned—they wished again they'd had just one more drink of water before going "on station." Odd, how throats could become dry, and stay so.

Arnold True, of the *Hammann*, "expected an attack." However, he was certain his was not "a feeling of doom," since "good Navy men always expect to win."

Five miles removed from the *Lexington*, Captain Elliott Buckmaster of the *Yorktown* was "ready and waiting." "Buck" Buckmaster, a tall, athletic Virginian thirty years out of the Academy, remained a formidable tennis opponent. The competitive spirit still surged within him.

Beck, aboard the squadron flagship *Phelps*, looked at the sky, whitecaps, talked to his meteorologist and decided that "the tables" were "reversed" from the day previous. In clearing weather the task force was now "out in the open."

At 0800 all crew mustered on stations. There were no absentees. "Sweepers!" were summoned by the familiar bos'n's whistle.

At 0820 "Ducky" Duckworth was given a report from one of his scout planes that two enemy cruisers and four carriers were bearing 006° or almost true north from the *Lexington*, 120 miles distant, speed 15 knots. The air officer noted: "Garble and interference prevented hearing plane's call. This also prevented checking of the reported bearing . . . the contact report was then repeated and received satisfactorily."

52

To Captain Sherman this was "thrilling news . . . the first sighting of the large Japanese carriers by either land-based or carrier planes."

Then Comtaskforce advised, "It is still very doubtful whether we are spotted."

In the next few minutes the *Lexington*'s commander was shown a "radio-intercepted transmission, from an enemy plane, giving our position, course and speed. We knew definitely we had been located."

Aboard the *Lexington* was an air-intelligence officer who could translate Japanese Kana as monitored.

Sherman then "predicted enemy attack would come in about 1100 and that it was possible for the carriers on both sides to be sunk by the simultaneous onslaught of the opposing air groups. We prepared to fight to the finish."

Jim Dudley assumed the watch. At general quarters or under battle alert the navigating officer took over the duties of the officer of the deck as "the immediate representative of the captain." Yeomen became telephone talkers on the many lines having an outlet on the bridge, affording the commanding officer links to all-important control stations in the ship.

Steering duties, recording duties and manning of all the auxiliary ship control stations were assumed by the quartermasters in the navigator's division. As a matter of fact, in place of the conventional helm or wheel, steering on the *Lex* was effected by a curious lever which, as Dudley had often thought, "seemed to have been stolen from an old-fashioned street car."

". . . 0850," continued the log, "turned into the wind at 20 knots and between 0907 and 0924 launched attack group, 13 VF (fighters), 11 VB (bombers), 12 VT (torpedo) and CAG (Commander Ault, commander air group) with 3 VS (scouts).

"Commander Air took tactical command."

Fitch, who was a naval aviator, was in command now until the emergency passed. The surface ships would be

May 8, the *Lex* "prepared to fight to the finish."

maneuvered only in close coordination with the needs of the air squadrons.

Everything looked "all right" to Duckworth, who added, "since the distance to the enemy was so great—180 miles— I personally told Lieutenant [Noel] Gayler [acting commander of the fighters in his superior's absence, already aloft] to make the trip if gasoline permitted, and that his presence over the enemy carrier would be of considerable value even if he did not do much fighting."

The dive bombers took off 30 gallons light of their 250-gallon capacities. However, they were carrying 1,000-pound bombs. Besides, the air officer figured 220 gallons was "more than enough fuel to permit them to travel the distances involved."

Gayler, from Birmingham, Alabama, had flown off "about 0910, some forty minutes after the initial contact. The reasons for all that delay was that the first contact reports were garbled. At the time of the takeoff the distance to the enemy was estimated as about 175 miles, and that's all the navigational dope we fighters had.

"The original plan was for the scout bombers to get their altitude gradually on the way over and work up to 18,000 feet, and for the torpedo planes to stay at a moderately low altitude of about 6,000 feet . . . the weather in our own disposition was good. We could see our own ships twenty-five or thirty miles away.

"However, as we progressed to the northeast, the weather became progressively poor, with rain squalls down to the surface."

Finally, the scout bombers became separated from the fighters.

Dudley instructed his quartermaster, Lester Sidney Hole, at 0930 to log, "went to general quarters and material condition ZED," the locking and "buttoning up" of the carrier.

From all over there echoed the slam and bang of massive steel doors. "Dogged down," they separated the huge ship into 600 compartments, as watertight as mechanically possible. Even so, after the fate of the *Titanic* in 1912, and

56

of other superships in the twentieth century, including the loss of the battle cruiser *Hood* in 1940, none dared claim any vessel "unsinkable."

At this time, too, another enemy reconnaissance plane was shot down, just as had happened the previous morning. "A great column of smoke on the horizon," was sighted from the signal bridge.

Sherman believed it "possible that the Japanese might have headed south and passed us during the night. Our planes covered 360 degrees of the compass, 150 miles to the south and 300 miles to the north. All hands were tense as we waited for the decisive action we were sure the day would bring."

Swept up by the headiness of the moment, Chaplain Markle asked permission to remain on the bridge in order to see what was going on. The chaplain had stayed "below decks at my battle station on all previous engagements with the enemy."

The wish was granted provided the minister "found a steel helmet to wear." But since Markle could not readily locate an extra, he "went to my battle station in the sick bay and reported to Commander White." Dr. Arthur J. White, a portly, rather reserved six-footer, the senior medical officer on the carrier, was well along in his career as naval surgeon.

The chaplain was not the only one whose instincts of self-preservation, curiosity and excitement had vied within him. Harold R. Littlefield, a Radioman 1st Class from Port Angeles, Washington, where he was a "ham" operator—W7DGY, in an electronic milieu where numbers and letters replace first or even last names—enjoyed his station "up in the forward superstructure three decks below the bridge."

If not the safest, it was a natural vantage point.

Harold was placed there near the secret radar shack since he was a maintenance man. He had found "so many bugs" in this wonderful new equipment that neither he nor his fellow technicians ever "did succeed in getting it to function properly."

Quite literally, there was standing room only in the main

57

radio compartment. Crowding in, leaning against the panels that were hot to the touch as well as with high voltage, operators as well as gunnery officers waited to relay minute-by-minute ranges and sight-settings.

Another radioman, John S. Wood, of Trout Lake, Washington, did not command either this "elite" area or a roost aloft. Even as in the Army, there always had to be replacements on instant call. When the alarm sounded, Wood's post was his own living quarters below the flight deck, port side, on standby. All Wood witnessed was the same limited foreground of gray bulkheads, with their layers of paint accumulated over the years, metal chairs, a couple of desks and four narrow bunks.

John Wood, a wiry young man and a member of the fleet boxing team, was in K division. He normally copied weather transmissions in the main radio shack. Although some five circuits were guarded around-the-clock, wireless was a one-way street for the most part, limited to receiving.

For that matter, the task force, endeavoring to maintain radio silence, was far more conscientious than the enemy. The Japanese persisted in the illusion that the Imperial Navy code had not been broken.

During the next half hour fourteen planes returned for fueling as the carrier, according to Captain Sherman, "prepared to fight to the finish." All emergency posts were fully manned and were in communication with every compartment, control station, battery and lookout perch on the long carrier.

Central station, or control, was the heart of general quarters, which was itself the most acute of all conditions at sea. The zeal, alacrity and efficiency with which general quarters was carried out could mean life or death to a ship and all souls aboard. By the same biological analogy, the bridge with its communications and navigation complex became the nerve center.

Three decks below the flight deck, this important damage-control post filled a broad room, or "space" stretching from port to starboard, almost a beam's width. Its principal furniture consisted of one long table, flanked by chairs for the twenty-some officers and men assigned to the compartment, at the sounding of general quarters.

Unlike the bridge, the area was relatively bare of navigation instruments, other than inclinometers to measure degree and direction of list, a small compass and an RPM, or revolutions-per-minute dial for the propellers. Standard and the most vital equipment here was the telephone, as indispensable as a doctor's stethoscope, supplemented by boards and pins.

Through telephones, the twenty men not only maintained instant communication with every recess of the ship—from forepeak, high in the bow, to the final decking above the rudder post—but could relay instantly intelligence and also commands to the vessel's five emergency repair parties. Each repair unit was comprised of 100 men, built around a nucleus of experienced shipfitters, carpenters, firemen, electricians, welders, metalsmiths and a carrier's several other mechanical ratings.

From the hush of this operating-theater-like room, bathed in bright blue light, firefighters could be dispatched instantly at the first cry of alarm. Emergency steering or electrical generating could be switched in, or ballasting rearranged to remove a sudden list and put the ship back in trim. Tom Nixon was the assistant damage-control officer, reporting to an officer who was scant less than worshiped—"Pop" Healy.

Lieutenant Commander Howard Raymond Healy, classmate of Duckworth's, Annapolis, 1922, was a short, heavyset native of Chelsea, Massachusetts. "Pop" Healy's pug face tended to mask the brains, ability and humanity that rested deep within.

"He never raised his voice," Nixon could recall with wonder. "When the going got tough, when you wanted something done, 'Pop' Healy first came to mind. He was a hero everyday. Any one of us would have gone to hell for 'Pop.'"

But no one really expected he'd have to, at least not this day, ominous as the immediate future may have appeared.

For at least one booster to morale, central station was snugly protected by fuel-oil and water-storage tanks mattressed against the ship's lengthy bulkhead bastions, plus the six inches of armor deck immediately above.

At 1000 hours, with sweepers already "piped down," supply was ordered to "break out the sandwiches" and distribute them along with fruit to the battle stations, "in lieu of regular noonday meal."

"About twelve 10-gallon milk cans with water were placed in passageway forward of the officers' galley," logged Lieutenant W. B. Durant, assistant supply officer.

This was all part of a culinary equivalent to damage control: "commissary control." It consisted of thirty-two ship's cooks and bakers, together with the battle reserve pool of forty-one men from sister departments. Battle reserve's function was to furnish replacements for casualties in the gun crews, repair parties or ammunition trains—directed, always, from "Pop" Healy's deep wellspring of critical command.

Aviators, if they sensed any appetite, and others in the air department, could enjoy limited cafeteria service—limited because most of the galley staff were already at general quarters posts or waiting in "battle reserve."

Men must eat, or at least know where the food and drink supply is, in or out of action. Unlike the British Navy, however, officers and men on the *Lexington* did not necessarily have to shower and don fresh clothing before anticipated action—as a preventative of infection. As United States Navy surgeons would aver, "our personnel are supposed to be clean *all* the time!"

6

". . . unidentified planes bearing 020°"

". . . 0957." logged Quartermaster Hole for Dudley, "changed speed to 15 knots."

All departments of the ship soon knew what was going on across the Coral Sea. Those who were not situated at a vantage point heard Chaplain Markle's intermittent announcements, like some sea-going radio commentator.

"Our planes," Lieutenant Charles M. Williams, a supply officer, would recall, "had picked up a Jap carrier, leaving just a relatively small number of aircraft to defend the task force. We put our last planes out to meet them.

"Our prayers were really with those boys, especially the ones in the planes that had been out on the long search. We could see the outline of the fight on the horizon because of several big plumes of smoke apparently about ten miles out as planes smacked into the sea."

All the ships of the task force were rigging for battle. Aboard the *New Orleans,* sick bay was counting flasks of blood plasma, bandages and medicine bottles in first-aid lockers.

"The sick men in the cots were serious and silent," Chaplain Forgy noticed. "Some of them turned on their sides and cocked their ears to pick up any threat of scuttlebutt that might pass through the lips of the busy men moving about the room. One lad, who had undergone an appendectomy the previous day, was so bothered by gas pains that it was obvious he didn't care whether the ship was afloat or sunk.

"Old Busby, the telephone talker, adjusted his earphones a dozen times as he balanced his chair on its two rear legs and tilted it back against the bulkhead. Suddenly he stopped fidgeting with the receivers and listened. He turned his head to a slight angle and stared unseeing into space as though to clear his mind of all but the message from topside."

In similar "country" aboard the *Lexington,* familiarly pungent with carbolic, Dr. Roach was hoping, with scant-suppressed enthusiasm, to "repeat our attack" of the previous day.

A few decks above the medical officer, Sherman observed that "the weather in the vicinity of the enemy was typical of the tropical front we had experienced the previous day, flyable but full of rain squalls offering good hiding places for surface ships trying to avoid an air attack."

Although the two air groups became "hopelessly separated," the *Yorktown's* planes first found the "Orange" forces at 10:32, according to Sherman's own log. He added:

"The two enemy carriers, they reported, had separated so that they were now some six or eight miles apart, with one group making for a rain squall and the other heading into the easterly wind and launching its planes. The *Yorktown* group at 10:58 A.M. dived down in a coordinated attack on the latter carrier.

"Enemy fighters attacked the bombers during their dives, and our pilots were hampered by fogging of bomb sights and windshields. Nevertheless, they claimed six sure hits which started fires aboard the carrier. Unmolested, the torpedo craft loosed their 'tin fish.'

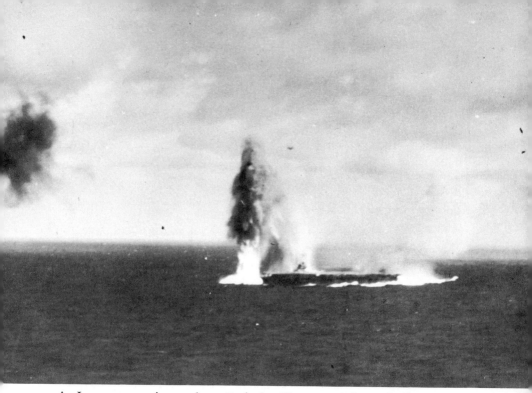

A Japanese carrier under attack by Navy torpedo and dive-bombing planes. NATIONAL ARCHIVES

"When the *Lexington* group, minus the dive-bombing squadron, arrived at the spot where they expected to find the enemy, nothing was in sight but rain squalls."

Noel Gayler, among the *Lexington* "group," noted they "had run out to the end of our navigational leg. We were in very poor weather and no sign of the Japs. So Commander Ault, who was the Group Commander, directed the torpedo plane commander by radio to fly a box. We turned 90° to the left, and after about two minutes on that leg came into a comparatively large clear area. Under the rain squalls on the far side of the area, say 20 miles away, we saw the Jap outfit. The first thing we saw was the smoke of some big ship burning. She had been attacked by the *Yorktown*'s air group. Then you could see the white wakes."

Gayler continued: "We immediately headed toward them. The group commander tried to get the bombers back in contact with us and directed the torpedo planes to circle and wait for them, so the attack could be coordinated, but without any success. The dive bombers never did find the target, and finally had to jettison their bombs and go home. The four dive bombers, led by the group commander, did attack, starting their dives from 2,500 feet.

"After about two minutes in this clear space, we were jumped by fighters from the Jap carriers. I should say there were possibly four or five Jap fighters.

"At first they were all air-cooled type Zeroes or some modification—it was the first I'd seen of them. Then after a minute or two of fighting a couple more fighters appeared on the scene that were liquid-cooled jobs that looked very similar to the ME 109F. I can't say definitely that that's what they were, but they were planes similar to them. Those planes I never saw take any real part in the action. All I saw was them coming at us. . . .

"We tangled with these people for a short while. I saw two of our fighters duck into a cloud; I can't account for the third plane that was with me. I was being chased and took cloud cover myself. I went on instruments in the general direction of the enemy fleet as I'd last seen it. I stayed in the clouds about three minutes and came out at about 1,000 feet directly over a Jap carrier, cruiser and destroyer—a total of three ships there.

"The carrier was by itself. I made two complete circles around it at about 1,000 feet. It either did not see me or did not take me under fire for some other reason. . . ."

And aboard the *Lexington,* by the quartermaster's log, "1044, on signal took special cruising disposition V . . . turned into wind and landed 3 SBD. All A.M. search groups returned. Resumed course 028°."

At the helm was Chief Quartermaster Frank "Pork Chops" McKenzie, an Alabaman and sixteen-year veteran in the service. Frank, who stood 5 feet, 6½ inches and weighed 180 pounds, was, like others of his rate, also a "bugle-master." He sounded the paternosters of a man-o'-war, from reveille through the day's complexities of routine calls and more strident alarms, and finally to taps, a sailor's "good night."

64

Confident that "we had made full preparations for the onslaught," and also "buttoned up the ship," Captain Sherman picked up his bull horn to shout something to a forward 1.1.-inch battery that had replaced the old 8-inch turrets. It was a direct way of transmitting orders, far faster, if perhaps less "reg" than the chain of command. However, when he spoke, nothing issued from the horn.

Annoyed, the captain crushed out his cigarette and had "Willie" Williamson, the electrical officer, summoned. His station was the forward electrical switch and instrument board, just across from central station, well removed from and below the bridge.

At 1048, logged "Red" Gill, the enemy "came straight in to intercept us, never disappearing from the screen, indicating that they flew out of the big null [no signal area] of our radar. This would place them up around 18,000 feet."

As Dudley would observe of this blind spot that permitted Japanese aircraft to fly in unobserved, "radar which had done so many wonderful things for us seemed to fail us when we needed it most."

Quartermaster Hole scribbled with mounting nervousness: "1057, guide of disposition shifted to *Yorktown* . . . unidentified planes bearing 020° distant 58 miles approaching."

Duckworth estimated the distance at fifty-two miles. Where warplanes were involved, however, a difference of six miles did not mean much.

According to Lieutenant Commander Edward J. "Jerry" O'Donnell, '29, from Dorchester, Massachusetts, the husky, tall gunnery officer in forward antiaircraft control, "these planes could not be seen. There were clouds and some haze along the port bow to the port beam. This information was sent to all stations, and the director and all port 5-inch guns were trained on the reported bearing."

Down in the engineer's battle-dressing station, amidst the sweltering, noisy firerooms, Dr. Roach listened to the loudspeaker's cry:

"Here they come!"

Then at once repeated, "Here they come!"

The same cry rang through the task force, ship after ship. Aboard the *New Orleans,* Chaplain Forgy heard the shout proclaiming unidentified aircraft:

"Bogies off the starboard!" (Contrasting with "skunks" for unidentified surface craft.)

Forgy continued: ". . . a hush throughout sick bay. We wondered whether these bogies would turn out to be some of the *Lex* planes or whether this was a real attack.

"A few moments later Busby called out again. This time he leaped to his feet. The front legs of his chair cluttered noisily to the steel deck behind him.

" 'Bogies identified as enemy planes! Stand by for action!'

"A half-dozen men about the ammunition hoist leaped to their feet and stood at their posts, waiting to grab the shells as they came up from the magazine below and transfer them to another hoist which would carry them to the batteries topside.

"I recalled that same hoist on December 7th. I was thankful we had power today and weren't helplessly tied up to a dock. The hum of the engines accelerated and I could feel the bow vibrating as the *No-Boat* strained every steel muscle in her body in this mad race to elude the enemy.

" 'How fast do you think we're going now?' I asked an old-timer at my side.

" 'Soon be making top speed.' [32 knots.]

"There was little comfort in it when we thought of the planes coming in at more than 200 miles per hour. Busby's voice barked again: 'Bandits! Coming in for attack!' [These were identified enemy aircraft.]

"Busby listened intently for a moment, then turned his head to the side and spoke quietly to the men near him. When he did this you always knew he was about to quote some of the conversation and by-play the talkers sandwich in on the wire between the official messages."

The *Lexington,* Sherman avowed, was "at 11 A.M. . . . as ready as humanly possible to give the enemy planes a hot reception and to withstand whatever damage we might suffer."

66

7

"The water . . . seemed full of torpedo wakes."

The prelude to and then the opening of the attack was seen, heard, felt and responded to in many ways by many persons in just as many separated portions of the carrier, above and below deck.

From "1101 to 1106," Quartermaster Hole logged, "launched 5 VF and 5 SBD. 1106 resumed course 028° (T). 1108 changed speed to 25 knots."

The carrier's guns, according to O'Donnell, "had barely reached the bearing when the first enemy torpedo plane was sighted on the port beam [at 1115]. Estimated range— 5,000 yards. The enemy was in a glide of about 10-15 degrees. Short-range weapons opened fire almost simultaneously with our sighting.

"He seemed to be making higher speed than our torpedo planes are accustomed to make. Although the automatic weapons fire against him did not look very effective, he kept veering away from it, to his left."

On the *New Orleans,* Chaplin Forgy "saw the cots quiver under the terrific snap of the 5-inch AA guns as our batteries began to bark. . . ."

Someone "up topside" thought he saw "about three planes burning and falling," but was unable to "tell whether they're ours or Japs."

The planes came in from out of the blinding sun. Then, as Lieutenant Williams, the supply officer, acting as a gunnery spotter observed, "they zoomed over the destroyer screen about 500 feet, then leveled out about fifty feet above the water coming in mighty fast."

O'Donnell continued:

"He dropped about 1,500 yards, in such a way that his torpedo was not released until after he had started his turn away; as a consequence his torpedo was well ahead of the ship, which had commenced its swing to the right. The torpedo plane attack developed from abaft the port beam as the ship swung right."

In Sherman's appraisal, the air fighting soon became "a melee":

"Our own planes were mixed in with the enemy and the sky was black with flak bursts. The Japanese spent no time in maneuvering, but dived straight in for the kill. The huge *Lexington* dwarfed the other ships in the formation and bore the brunt of the attack.

"It was beautifully coordinated. From my bridge I saw bombers roaring down in steep dives from many points in the sky, and torpedo planes coming in on both bows almost simultaneously. There was nothing I could do about the bombers, but I could do something to avoid the torpedoes.

"As I saw a bomb leave one of the planes, it seemed to be coming straight for where I stood on the bridge. Had I better duck behind the thin armored shield? If it had my name on it, I thought, there was no use dodging, and if not, there was no need to worry. At any rate, I had work to do to try to evade the torpedoes.

"The ideal way to drop torpedoes was for groups of planes to let go simultaneously on both bows. In this method, if the target ship turned toward one group to parallel its torpedoes, it presented its broadside to the other. The timing was vital. The enormous *Lexington* was very slow in turning. It took thirty to forty seconds just to put the rudder hard over. When she did start to turn, she moved majestically and ponderously in a large circle.

"As I saw the enemy torpedo planes coming in on both bows, it seemed to me that those to port were closer than those to starboard. They were approaching in steep glides, faster than we considered practicable for torpedo dropping.

"The air was full of antiaircraft bursts and the din was terrific. When the planes to port were about 1,000 yards away, I motioned to the helmsman, Chief Quartermaster McKenzie, for hard left rudder. It seemed an eternity before the bow started to turn—just as the enemy planes started disgorging their fish.

"The water in all directions seemed full of torpedo wakes."

To Stanley Johnston, the "wicked noses" of the Japanese torpedoes "looked like death incarnate," giving him the illusion "they are alive and breaking water to peek at us."

Coxswain Conley Cain, 128 feet up on the forward, starboard range finder, thought the torpedoes resembled nothing more animate than "telephone poles" streaking incongruously through the water. Cain, a Navy football player from Santa Fe and formerly aboard the *Neosho,* was too busy calling ranges to experience any particular emotion at the missiles coming for his ship.

"In less than a minute," Sherman continued, "the first torpedoes had passed astern. We quickly shifted rudder to head for the second group of planes. These split up to fire on both bows, the hardest maneuver for us to counter. Then it became a matter of wriggling and twisting as best we could to avoid the deadly weapons heading our way.

"I remember seeing two wakes coming straight for our port beam, and there was nothing I could do about them. The wakes approached the ship's side, and I braced myself for the explosion. Nothing happened.

"I rushed to the starboard bridge and there were the wakes emerging from that side. The torpedoes were running too deep and had passed completely under the ship.

"My air officer, Commander Duckworth, was on the bridge.

69

" 'Don't change course, captain!' he exclaimed. 'There's a torpedo on each side of us running parallel. If we veer we'll collect one sure!'

"We held our course with a torpedo fifty yards on either beam."

Sooner or later it was inevitable that the *Lexington* would "collect" one. Lester Sidney Hole's hand shook as he next wrote in the quartermaster's log: "1118, torpedo hit port side about frame 50."

This location was below the waterline slightly forward of the superstructure area of the carrier, although Duckworth thought it was somewhat farther along the length, "just at the forward elevator."

The torpedo raised up the *Lexington* as though she were "going over a hump," as it felt to Markle. Then the ship "lurched and shuddered. Men were staggering about and many were knocked off their feet." Included in this number was McKenzie, the helmsman, who quickly regained his balance, however.

In the sick bay, where Markle was standing, "everyone seemed calm. We thought that we would go through all right. However, as dust and smoke began to seep in, I realized I would need my gas mask. The senior surgeon told me to go ahead and get it."

Two minutes after the first torpedo slammed home, a second made "a heavy hit" on the same side, but more toward the beam.

Deep in the ship, at his engineer's battle-dressing station. Dr. Roach felt the concussion as "a rather dull, rumbling sort of explosion accompanied by a violent shaking of the ship."

Others within the *Lexington*'s vitals scarcely noticed anything at all, so great was the ship's bulk and capacity to absorb a few hundred pounds of high explosives.

Harold Williamson, back at his electrical board and awaiting opportunity to repair the captain's bullhorn, might not have been so concerned at the effects of the blast had it not belatedly occurred to him that he was sitting on a 1,000-

An enemy dive-bomber was just sweeping over a destroyer, leaning into a fast, evasive turn, and starting its run on the *Lexington* when this remarkable, hitherto unpublished photograph was made.

pound aerial bomb. (The bombs had to be stored all around the ship, wherever there was room for the bulky objects.) He started to get up as though, *now,* this was an exceptionally hazardous roost. Then he was made aware of a physical reaction hitherto unknown to him. His feet, at first, would not respond.

Tom Nixon, in central station, perceived a "dull thud which jolted the ship comfortably."

From his "beautiful vantage point," Radioman Littlefield heard a man beside him shout, "We've been hit!" Then the thought occurred to him, "just as though he didn't know it as well as myself."

Conley Cain noticed a singular effect. Rust or possibly flakes of red lead shaken loose covered the deck at his feet around the mount, like "red dust."

71

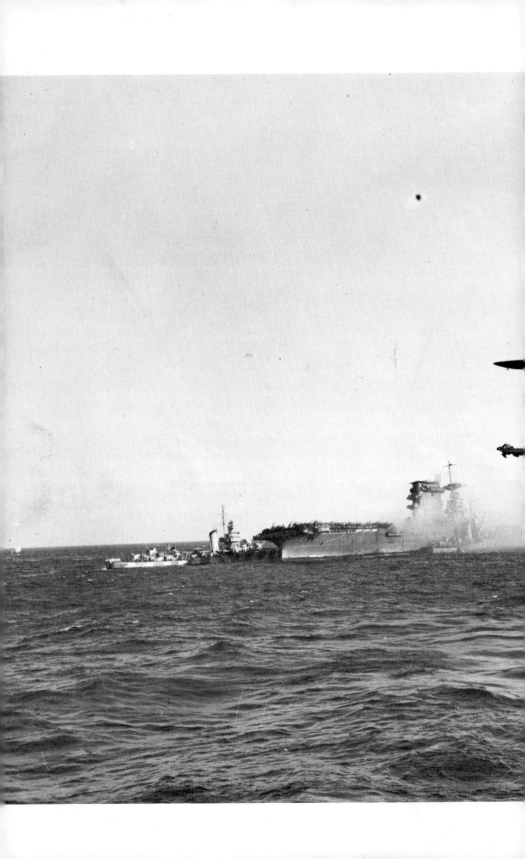

Fred T. Hartson, AMM2C.

"The *Lex* has been hit."

Dudley, whose prime duty now was to see that "every wish of the captain as to control of the ship was immediately executed," nonetheless could not observe what was going on. A brass canopy restricted vertical visibility, although he could see what the ships of the task force were doing and observe the "splashes and flame from hits and near misses."

One telephone circuit from the bridge was connected to the forepeak, where two men were stationed to warn of undersea sounds.

"They showed a lively interest," according to Dudley, "also imagination. They were shouting encouragement to the gunners like spectators at a boxing match: 'Give 'em hell! Hit 'em again! Don't let 'em up!' "

Stanley Johnston, standing beside Captain Sherman, turned to him to assert, "I think it's going to be all right, captain. . . ." And the two shook hands.

The byplay evoked a wry glance from Quartermaster McKenzie who clutched the steering lever with something like a death grip.

Len Olliff, still without his shower or "sack time," took shelter in the photo lab since he was assigned no general-quarters station. He figured he might as well remain there "until the show was over."

Other "mechs" not aloft with their planes were caught on the open deck and found no hiding place. James V. "Frenchy" Landis, who had studied for the priesthood as a boy in France, then joined the Navy as an aviation machinist mate, "ran around like mad," trying to find some sort of bulwark against bombs and shrapnel.

Fred Hartson, who admitted to a long-standing "touch of claustrophobia," was less afraid of experiencing an attack on deck than being closeted below. When his plane was tethered at the parking edge, he slept by choice in its bomb bay. With the addition of a blanket, it was not uncomfortable.

Pressed hard against the stack's dubious protection, Fred, "a boy from a hick town," mused, "Where do they get the authority to hurt this ship?"

74

Then, after a glance, he wondered, "Where did our cruisers go?"

He found himself staring at "Jap torpedo planes, 360° around the carrier." He looked into the face of one of the planes as it swept across the deck.

From slightly better cover on the *Lexington*'s island, Lieutenant Williams watched apparently the same foe:

"One of them came in. I saw at least four streams of fire going toward it. They seemed like they had him completely boxed, but he came right through it.

"He banked, dropped his fish—just sort of a little splash—about 600 yards out. He came roaring right on in at our battery. He had the insolence to bank again, about twenty feet in front of us, then just sort of stood on end and roared up along the ship. Perhaps he was trying to distract fire from the ones that were coming in behind him, and he did it because our gunners, in spite of the fact that they shouldn't have fired on him probably after he dropped his torpedo, should have gone after the others coming in.

"They just couldn't resist the temptation and turned him over. Four or five streams of fire hit him, turned him over, right on over as he was still in that bank, propped him on his back. By the time he got back to us again he was just a patch of gasoline burning on the water beneath us and we didn't have much time to worry about him though.

"Another one came in right behind him, a little to the side, started smoking about 200 yards out, caught fire about a hundred yards out and hit the ship right below number 1 battery."

Duckworth, with his pilot's eye, realized the enemy torpedo plane had executed "a double snap roll" and crashed into the water just under the flare of the mighty port bow, although it missed the ship herself.

Before the aircraft disappeared "in a clap of thunder and fire," Captain Sherman noticed a torpedo still slung to its underside, "a peculiar wooden framework around the missile's nose and propeller mechanism." He figured it was a

75

"cushioning device" to allow the torpedoes to be dropped at high speed without "excessive shock to the delicate machinery."

Down in his compartment, John Wood, the radioman, was "just plain scared," as he crouched against unyielding deck plates and bulkhead.

"It sounded like all the guns in the Navy were going . . . a piece of shrapnel came through the bulkhead.

"I lived my life over, a dozen times. I thought of the games I sometimes played with my twin brother . . . the *Lexington* lurched, then settled down."

On the *New Orleans,* Chaplain Forgy, even as Radioman Wood, was finding it "a lot harder to take a battle below-decks," adding:

"You can't see what's going on, you don't know where the enemy is and there is nothing you can do to release the dammed-up emotions multiplying inside your mind. I looked out at the sweating men at the ammunition hoist and envied them. They were keeping busy and their minds were on their jobs—not filled with flashes of fear and uncertainty.

"Dr. Evans waved us down and shouted something. You couldn't hear any words over the ear-splitting banging of the guns, but we knew his order without hearing it. We all lay flat, hugging the deck. Some of the corpsmen crawled under cots. Others snuggled against the bulkheads for added protection.

"I lay there with my face against the cool steel deck and looked through the doorway at the ammunition crew. The men were working like parts of a well-lubricated machine as they grabbed each shell and pushed it through a hole in the bulkhead to the men at the next hoist. I wondered how they could maintain that back-breaking pace without missing or dropping a shell.

"The guns above us were firing so rapidly now that the deck beneath me shook continuously. It slapped back and forth against my cheek.

"Dozens of thoughts and half-thoughts raced through my mind. I looked up at the overhead and wondered what I would do if we were hit. If an armor-piercing bomb found us, I thought, it would probably come through the quarter-deck, the main deck, and let go right here. Maybe one of those Jap planes had already sent a torpedo at us. Well, down here we'd never know until it hit. I wondered how I could get out of here if we did take a hit and the water began to pour in. Odd, I never thought of that before. A fellow should always think of how he can get out of places in an emergency.

"There was no letup in the barking of the guns topside. It was almost a continuous roar now, like a huge machine gun with the trigger held down.

"I looked across the room to one of the boys in the cots. He reached under his pillow and pulled out a little blue ring box. In it was a diamond he had bought at Honolulu to give to his girl back in the states. I knew he was wondering now whether he would ever live through this to see the girl he wanted for his wife."

On the *Lexington,* Chaplain Markle reached his cabin and obtained "gas mask, flashlight and penknife. I ran at once to the passageway amidships where I found four men who were nearly naked yelling for help, having been horribly burned. One Filipino cook [or steward] was there in the passageway just aft of the officers' head [toilet] about frame 20 on the main deck, and he helped me get the men on the cots in the passageway and take off the remainder of their clothes and give them a drink of water and a morphine injection.

"I then ran back to my room to call Dr. White and report the conditions I found on the main deck. Dr. White advised me to remain on the main deck and assist the wounded, which I did."

In the yet unchecked fury and confusion of it all, "Red" Gill heard a *Yorktown* pilot radioing plaintively: "What are you shooting at me for? What have I done *now?*"

8

". . . about Louise and the baby."

The *Lexington*'s batteries hammered away so fast that Gunner's Mate G. M. Harden confessed, "I could not hear my own gun. I could only tell when it fired by watching the recoil."

This blanking out of sound was also reported by Stanley Johnston: "There's so damned much noise I can't hear any single explosion, almost like a complete silence." In fact, there was such an abundance of this paradoxical brand of "silence" that O'Donnell reported, "I cannot be certain of the order of the attack."

Duckworth, the air officer, had a grandstand perspective, "on the port side of the bridge at air control, with a full and unobstructed view." He continued:

"At 1120½, several torpedoes were observed approaching on the port quarter. The ship had stopped swinging right and was started left. I called to the captain to go back to the right because there were more torpedoes coming. This he did.

"Two of the approaching torpedoes broached about 100 yards out. One resumed its depth and struck the ship at the stem. It didn't do any real damage. The other continued on the surface and passed clear. Two others passed about 100 to 200 feet ahead.

"These last four torpedoes approached the ship from broad on the port quarter. Two others appeared running deep from just abaft the beam and passed under the ship between the forward elevator and number 2 gun gallery. Another torpedo appeared from broad on the port beam and struck a little aft of the forward elevator.

"The first three or four torpedoes were dropped from about 1,000 yards, but after that the drops were outside of 3,000 yards. I believe that the effectiveness of our AA fire was responsible for this, as I saw about three of the first torpedo planes shot down.

"Several of the torpedo planes were noticed streaming gasoline as they flew past, indicating they had been hit."

At 1122, according to Quartermaster Hole, another torpedo hit, somewhat forward, also on the already hurting port side.

"It didn't throw us off our feet," according to Lieutenant Williams, the supply officer. "It was just sort of a big balloon, and then a tremendous geyser of water and oil rose in the air. As we moved foward at about 30 knots, our gun platform stuck out from the side of the ship and the geyser settled down on us. We thought we were sinking.

"It was a solid wall of water and covered the whole battery with about a foot of oil and water. Before we had time to dig ourselves out from that, somebody yelled, "Dive bombers!"

Still on the flight deck near a 5-inch 25 battery but with no sure place to hide, Hartson was drenched completely by this quasi-tidal wave.

The *Lexington* had swallowed a minimum of three and a maximum of five torpedoes—as variously counted by those aboard—in the four-minute period between 1118 and 1122. Still, she could churn ahead at the 30 knots estimated by the excited and now drenched supply officer, Williams. But "Pop" Healy down in central station thought the carrier's luck should not be pressed.

"If you take any more torpedoes," he advised the bridge, "take them on the starboard!"

All so far had smashed into the port side.

Healy's suggestion seemed very amusing to Dudley, standing next to Duckworth. He commenced to laugh.

Duckworth, although he could wonder at what might be so funny, concluded that the carrier would be heading for "a real navy yard overhaul." The idea, the half-hope had flashed through the minds of others as well, all except for a small minority who had already abandoned hope.

In his quarters well below, John Wood remained convinced that "in any instant . . . it will all be over."

A "talker" on the intercom next to "Rip" Raring at the air operations station also despaired within the aerologist officer's hearing. Life at the moment was looking very perilous.

Few proved as phlegmatic as Lester Jones, a sturdy seaman from Jacksonville, Florida, who admitted that getting sunk or even hurt were considerations farthest from his thoughts. A pointer on a rapid-firing gun, Jones nonetheless was annoyed when shrapnel pierced the water jacket and drained the weapon of cooling fluid.

The bombers, although they admittedly produced something akin to a negative reaction in Jones, were still frightening to most men. The enemy torpedo planes, by their mission, were more impersonal. They were after an inanimate object: the ship herself.

Bombs, even as the doughboys of World War I believed, all seemed to hurtle down bearing someone's name. They were like the gun barrels of a firing squad. One wanted to duck and hide, ostrich-like.

Lieutenant (jg) Grant Hansen, a reserve signal officer, catching Stanley Johnston about to dodge below the canvas spray shield on the bridge, wryly remarked, "It's not even waterproof, won't so much as keep out the spray!"

To Ensign Edward "Ed" Muhlenfeld of Baltimore, at 6′7″ the tallest man on board, the bombs plummeting toward his forward gun station looked "as big as beer barrels." To others, the missiles resembled ugly-snouted "pigs."

One of the first bombs appeared to have sliced through the whistle cord on the funnel, starting a continuous "deafening scream."

Vernon Highfill, the fireman who had decided in the opening moments of the attack that "hell" had broken loose, was at his control station trying to maintain oil and water pressure as well as vacuum for the generators when "I got a call over the J.V. [auxiliary] phone to shut off steam to the siren and whistle because some of the men on the smoke stack were getting hurt with steam.

"I had to run through Baker unit room and up the ladder to shut off the steam. I returned to my battle station."

Dudley, the navigator, who found the din "absolutely deafening," held his own theories about the stuck siren. He thought that a sort of "humping" of the ship beneath the bridge from the torpedo hit simply had "stretched the siren pull wire."

Whatever the cause of the runaway siren, the capping of the eerie bedlam came "as a relief to our eardrums," as Harold Littlefield, as close as anyone to it, voiced the sentiments of many, if not the majority.

Another bomb exploded against the stack. Although not large, it virtually obliterated a battery of .50-caliber machine guns emplaced precariously on a narrow, protruding balcony. A second ensign with this unlucky battery—group 4, composed largely of Marines—assumed control after the ranking ensign had been killed, along with five others.

A few of the crew still on the flight deck had seen a puff of dirty yellow smoke beside the funnel, then "great clouds of smoke or soot from the stack." They guessed what had happened.

Among the watchers was a machinist mate 3d, Joe D. Hart Jr., from Macon, Georgia, a plane captain (or maintenance "boss") in Olliff's squadron. Joe, who had remained with his waiting bomber during the attack, was among those with an immediate kin on board: Tom, a younger brother. Joe, starting his third year in the Navy, had last spoken to Tom, a seaman, when the latter was leaving for his general quarters station on the .50-caliber group 4 guns.

Tom, who had requested assignment to the *Lexington* because of his brother, had been at Pearl Harbor on December 7. This morning the younger Hart had mentioned something to the effect that it looked like he'd be "seeing some more excitement."

Joe Hart squinted toward the stack and had "a funny feeling." Then he decided to find a safer refuge than the flight deck, since he noticed strafings that pocked the teak flooring.

This "stitching" effect along the flight deck had also been observed by Duckworth from his higher elevation. Moments before, the air officer had been wondering, "How come with all those strafing runs their bullets aren't hitting the ship?"

Hart now raced to one of the old 8-inch turrets, where the replacement 1.1's were barking without cease, and slid under the overhang. Joe, having picked up more momentum than he had estimated, tumbled into a dry-fire-chemical can, which burst like a sack of flour.

For a moment he sat there, stunned and covered with the white extinguishing material. He thought, "I guess this'll get us to Australia and time off." Then he began brushing away the white powder.

Lieutenant "Red" Coward, at sky aft, was focusing his thoughts on Bremerton, Washington, where he would wait out the "three months for repair" he estimated the *Lex* would require.

It was then that a young ensign at the outboard director turned without visible sign of injuries, opened his mouth as if to speak, then toppled over dead, at the gunnery officer's feet.

There were several officers stationed at this large battery

of 5-inch, 1.1-inch, 20-mm. and .50-calibers, all controlled by Coward with his phones, Mark 19 directors and altimeters. He expected casualties.

Max Price, directing his .50's in rapid fashion, all at once collapsed, as suddenly as had the other officer. The handsome member of the Class of '39 had been hit in the back of his head by a large chunk of shrapnel. He was dead.

Someone—Coward was not certain who—knelt and removed Max's collar bars, presumably to return them to his family.

Conley Cain, forward on the starboard range finder, looked at his opposite number on the port side, a coxswain from Seattle, just as he fell with a reddening shrapnel wound staining his waist. "I had to watch him lying there, bleeding to death. There was nothing I could do!"

As on the bridge, the gun director's only shield was canvas.

Five miles abeam of the *Lexington,* the *Yorktown* was ducking bombs and torpedoes like an adept end runner on a gridiron. While she was not as fast as the *Lexington,* her turning circle was half that of the older carrier: 1,000 yards, or less.

Captain Buckmaster possessed every reason for gratification. By standing on the bridge in the open, he recalled, he was "able to see the splashes of the torpedoes when they were dropped. By turning away at flank speed and paralleling the direction of the drop, I was lucky enough to avoid all of them."

Hartwig, on the *Russell,* was understandably impressed by Buckmaster for doing "a terrific job of avoiding."

The *Yorktown*'s commander saw "several" torpedoes passing on each side of the ship, "close aboard," and traveling faster than the carrier, just underneath the relatively clear water. Her luck ran out, however. The *Yorktown* could not duck bombs as readily or facilely as she could torpedoes.

A 500-pounder penetrated the flight deck and exploded in a storeroom underneath. Thirty-seven men died instantly, and almost as many more were badly hurt. The *Yorktown*'s water-line was also pocked with holes and dents from near misses.

Captain Sherman glanced at the other carrier, "off in the distance to the southeastward." He observed "a column of black smoke rising from her flight deck."

Curiously, "Red" Gill, the fighter director, was just about to suggest the temporary switching of "direction control"—radio communication with the fighter planes—to the companion carrier. The *Lexington*'s was not working just right. Because of the *Yorktown*'s hit, however, Gill resolved to await repairs to the *Lexington*'s equipment.

The task force's aircraft, as a matter of fact, were doing very nicely with or without "direction control." Lieutenant Gayler had finished "tangling" with the Zeroes and was thinking about the return flight. He was short of gasoline, shorter as every second droned by.

"There were no other aircraft in sight," he would report. I stayed over the Jap [carrier] in the expectation that our torpedo planes would show up. Then I caught a glimpse of the other Japs—about fifteen miles east of me.

"There were a number of ships with one large vessel which I took to be a carrier burning and making quite a good deal of smoke. I decided that the TBD's had hit them instead, and went on back to the rendezvous point.

"The weather was so dirty I wasn't able to rendezvous with any of my own fighters or, as a matter of fact, to find any other planes at all. I could hear my other section leader calling on the radio, but I couldn't get him to answer me. So, after about four minutes I headed on back for our own disposition. I had only a very vague notion as to where I was because the only information I had of the enemy position was what I'd got by tracking our own TBD's on the way over, and I'd been fighting since then. But after about ten minutes I sighted one of our SBD's up ahead—it turned out to be Ensign [M. M.] Haschke, the only remaining member of the Group Commander's section.

"I found out that the Group Commander and his section,

a total of four planes, had hit one Jap carrier just before the torpedo planes hit it and had scored two 1,000 pound hits."

Attackers and attacked now were engaged in an arena covering thousands of square miles of the Coral Sea. Aboard the *New Orleans,* in a section where the Japanese appeared to hold the upper hand, Chaplain Forgy continued:

"Busby pushed the phones hard against his ears lest the din of battle drown out some important message. I looked around for Brookfield. I wondered how he was taking it.

"He was on one of the cots over in the corner, lying face down. I couldn't see his expression, but his hands were clenched tightly about the supporting chains. His knuckles were white. I wondered how his own battle was going, that terribly real mental battle he was fighting against fear. On the deck near him was *The Keys of the Kingdom,* dog-eared near the middle. I hoped that Brookfield had been able to get outside himself. . . .

"I thought about Louise * and the baby that was coming. I hoped it would be a boy, but I wondered whether I would be lucky enough to see him. Yes, it will be a him, I assured myself, and I prayed that I might live through this to see my son. I thought about Louise being alone with the baby if I didn't get through. It wasn't a pretty picture, and I tried to think of something else.

"Suddenly the guns ceased firing.

"We got up as one man and stretched. Our mouths were dry from the extreme nervous tension, just as on the day at Pearl Harbor.

"The boy with the gas pains called for water. His mouth was so void of moisture that the words were thick, almost incoherent. Brookfield leaped to his feet and hurried across the room to the side of the patient with a pitcher of ice water and a tumbler. He stuck a tube in the glass and handed it to him. I watched Brookfield closely as he moved from cot

---

* The former Louise Morgan, a choir singer from Murray, Kentucky, whom Forgy married before the war.

to cot, giving the men water and asking them what they needed.

"I felt better inside. I knew Brookfield was beginning to win his battle.

"The men crowded around Busby, pleading for some word of what had happened. Busby's face was serious and he spoke softly.

" 'The *Lex* has been hit,' he said.

"The room hushed. The *Lex,* good old *Lady Lex.* We prayed that it wasn't a bad hit.

"Busby's voice clipped through the air again: 'Bandits returning for another run! Stand by for action!'

"The deafening bang-bang-bang began once more as we dropped to the deck. Once again the handful of men at the hoist began their feverish work of speeding ammunition upward to feed the hungry AA guns that were barking angrily for more and more shells.

"The *No-Boat,* her engines throbbing wide open, rolled first to starboard, then to port. As the list of the deck under me changed rapidly, I knew we were zigzagging in a series of short, sharp turns. I wondered whether we were trying to dodge a dive-bomber that might at this second be roaring down at us from the sky.

"Suddenly a dull thud slapped against the hull of the vessel. The great cruiser bounced. Then she rolled into a heavy list to port. I spread my legs and braced my hands against the slanting deck to keep from sliding across the room."

9

". . . trying to keep from going crazy."

From the bridge of the *Phelps,* Beck studied the hurt *Lexington* and thought "to see her in agony was most depressing."

Aboard another destroyer, the *Russell,* Roy Hartwig experienced "an awful sick feeling" in the pit of his stomach watching the carrier being "immobilized." He judged that she was "just too doggone big" and ponderous to maneuver, a target not easy to miss—especially by the concerted effort of 100 planes, which apparently was the number hurled at her today by the foe.

Even so, Commander "Beany" Jarrett, of the *Morris,* thought the task force would be putting up a better defense if the gunnery were better, Without proximity fuses, the shells just never "seemed to catch up with their targets . . . couldn't hit a damn thing."

The pilot of a Navy plane, apparently out of gas and arriving back during the melee, crash-landed near the *Morris.*

"For Christ's sake!" shouted Captain Gilbert C. "Gib" Hoover, commanding Destroyer Squadron 2, "don't stop!"

Jarrett did not intend to do so. He knew full well that the aviator, relatively secure in his Mae West lifejacket, would soon be rescued by one of the destroyer screen specifically detailed for this duty.

He was also spotted by Captain Sherman, watching through his binoculars, who saw the pilot waving. The *Lexington*'s commander tapped a signalman on the shoulder and told him to flash to a destroyer astern: "Pick that boy up!"

The carrier now showed a 6° port list. This in all probability was caused by flooding from one or two of the more serious torpedo hits. It was the function of those in central station to attempt to remove this list by redistributing the fuel and water ballast.

The dive bombers continued to hurl themselves down, seconds apart, in chain formation. Most of the missiles hit in the carrier's wake.

Stanley Johnston watched "the bombs leave each plane. The aircraft followed, gradually flattening out. Their machine guns and wing cannon winked momentarily. . . ."

Robert Griffith, a machinist mate whose duty was the upkeep and operation of the flight deck arresting gear, continued to stand in the open, "at the barriers located just at the aft end of the island structure." He wrote:

"I moved forward to get away from the concussion of the 1.1 battery, and sat on deck with my back against the stack housing. I could see the planes making their runs from the port side. The USS *Yorktown* was on our starboard.

"I could see the bombs coming down and passing over the stack and see the torpedo planes making their runs."

Sherman wrote: "Five bombs had landed on the *Lexington*. One bomb hit the port gallery just outside the admiral's cabin [on the main deck, just below the flight deck, ahead of the 'island']. It wiped out most of the gun crews in that vicinity and started fires. In addition, it killed Commander Gilmore, our paymaster, and Commander Wadsworth Trojakowski, our dentist, who were in the passageway just inboard, and communications men in an adjacent [coding] room.

90

"Bombs started fires in other parts of the ship, but none was especially serious. Fragments killed men in one of the fire-control stations aloft."

Lieutenant Williams had a narrow escape. Ensign R. H. "Bob" Zwierschke of the Supply Corps, who had just relieved Williams at the coding board located at general quarters in the admiral's cabin, was mortally wounded. Gilmore, curiously, showed no signs of injury, leading Dr. White to conclude that the paymaster had succumbed to a concussion.

"The bomb," executive officer "Mort" Seligman estimated, "was at least 500, perhaps 1,000 pounds. . . . Part of the 5-inch ammunition in the 'ready' locker in the admiral's cabin detonated, which added to the destruction. Fire started on the gun platform and swept through the cabin and surrounding area."

Chaplain Markle, summoned by the chief surgeon, arrived at the devastated area where he "found a hospital corpsman administering tannic acid jelly to the patients and generally caring for the wounded.

"They were horribly burned. Their clothing and shoes had been almost blasted from them and some were almost naked . . . these men kept coming from the 5-inch gun batteries, sometimes alone and others with the help of a shipmate.

"Some had burned eyes and had to be led through the passageway. I took charge and got them stretched out on cots. The senior surgeon sent equipment and a pharmacist's mate to assist. We greased them with tannic acid, and gave injections of morphine to those in great pain, marking a red cross on their foreheads with Mercurochrome so no one would give them another injection.

"There was chaos and turmoil, smoke and fumes, bedlam. . . . I went out to the gun galleries to see where the men had been coming from. The 1,000-pound bomb had wiped out one whole gun crew and part of another.

"I saw a Marine captain pacing up and down. He had stacked the bodies of the dead against a bulkhead and had cleared away debris and seen that hot ammunition was tossed overboard. He had the third gun ready for action. The bodies were charred beyond recognition, frozen grotesquely in whatever position they happened to be standing in when the bomb hit.

"I made a search through officers' country [quarters] for other people and found several who had been killed instantly, and two who had been asphyxiated. Some were so mutilated it was impossible to identify them. I went aft to see how other parts of the ship were faring."

Markle "administered first aid, artificial respiration" to Gilmore "but to no avail—he apparently was dead when we found him. We covered him with a door curtain and left him beside two other bodies in the main deck passageway by the entrance to the coding office."

According to Duckworth, "one of the bombs hit just aft of the port beam about fifty yards out. It was about one-half second delayed action and only threw up spray about fifty feet high. Most of the bombs went over. One 1,000-pound near-miss was received close aboard just under the 20-mm. guns in the gig boat pocket.

"One of the last bombs released struck the side of the ship at the after end of the number 2 gun gallery. I thought it was delayed action armor-piercing, for the resulting hole was small. I was watching all releases and ducked behind my splinter shield on this one. The explosion raised the flight deck about six inches in the vicinity of the jagged hole.

"The bomb had hit the fire outlet on the gun gallery, so we ran hoses across the flight deck. The Amdyco—dry chemical [to be mixed with water into solution]—didn't seem to help much, although there was no flame appearing on the flight deck. I believe the Marines put the fire out below deck with hoses."

Dr. Roach, in the heat of the engineer's battle-dressing station, had been listening to the boom and echo of the torpedo and bomb concussions as they vibrated and shook through the carrier's vitals.

"The first of these shocks came as rather dull, rumbling explosions accompanied by a violent shaking of the ship. In

92

Gun crews were wiped out, victims were burned beyond recognition.

all, there were probably four explosions, which we thought to be torpedoes. These were followed almost immediately by several very loud, sharp blasts, which we presumed to be bombs.

"A few moments later smoke appeared through our ventilating shaft. We knew then, of course, that the ship had been hit, but we also knew our firerooms were functioning perfectly, or at least satisfactorily, as we could hear those blowers turning up at full speed.

"We also could feel the motion of the ship through the water, so that we down below felt that all was well.

"Of course, the ship was constantly changing course and rolling quite heavily. As torpedoes or bombs would hit, the lights would momentarily flick out but always came back on again."

Lieutenant Williams, at his own battery, admitted he was mostly "trying to keep from going crazy and trying to keep from turning and running because all the planes in the neighborhood were Japs. . . ."

He could "never forget that little gunner on number 3 gun who looked like a dead-end kid himself, sort of a lobe-eared and had such bad teeth I don't see how he ever got in the Navy. To make matters even worse he had a shaved head.

"When the dive-bomber was coming in—looked like he was going right down my throat—his ammunition man standing right beside him had frozen stiff. Well, this little gunner was standing on one foot firing, holding onto this 20-mm. and kicking the hell out of his ammunition bearer with his other foot. He got results, too."

Lieutenant Hoyt Mann, a lean Alabaman, was among the few pilots "sweating out" the attack in the combination ready room-wardroom, with only two "talkers" to relay what was happening from the intercom. He had been the last to land before the enemy came in and "since the topside gas had been secured, I could not be gassed for takeoff."

Mann, a star tennis player and choir singer of the Class of '36, had been aware of the sound of guns, the "crunch" of several torpedoes and then had balanced himself against what he felt to be a "small list to port."

There had been "nervousness" but "no panic" until "suddenly we heard a very loud explosion and were swept from our feet by flame and smoke pouring into the wardroom:" He continued:

"It became very apparent that we had to get to open air quick—smoke, dust and all the lights gone. Fortunately, we were in officers country, and having been aboard since 1939 I knew the place by heart.

"We got everyone together and hanging onto each other's coattails started for the nearest exit topsides. After much stumbling in the darkness [over what turned out to be the dead in passageways], we broke out onto the starboard AA platform, just as a new wave of torpedo planes was making its attack."

While Mann realized that his little group of pilots, stewards and others collected en route was "very much in the way of the laboring gun crews," they all "had air to breathe so were grateful to flatten ourselves against the bulkhead."

10

Seven Bells

The situation below was worsening. Lieutenant Commander Alexander F. Junker, the engineering officer from Pennsylvania, learned that the water was pouring into boiler rooms 2, 4, and 6—that is, three out of sixteen—and ordered them to "secure." "Heine" Junker reported: "Fireroom 2 had eighteen inches of water and oil, fireroom 4 had twelve feet, and fireroom 6 had five feet.

"Orders were given to secure the firemain in these firerooms, for it was suspected that these firerooms were flooding from ruptured firemains, fuel and feed water lines. This proved to be the case.

"A bilge suction was taken on these firerooms [which] all had minor leaks along the seams of the outboard bulkheads, and the bulkheads of the trunks leading to the firerooms were distorted and stove in, especially in 4 fireroom."

Junker, his subordinates attested, was a good officer, one who kept everyone "on his toes," a perfectionist in the engineering department. "Willie" Williamson remembered a three-day project, around the clock, to repair a burned-out electrical panel section.

At half-past eleven Junker's latest from engine "country" —main control—was logged on the bridge: "Report of damage gave boilers 2, 4 and 6 out of commission, speed reduced to 25 knots. Ready service ammunition after end number 2 gun gallery burning but fire there being extinguished. Ship turned to the right to be about 270° (T), steadying there momentarily, then continued turn to the right to come into the wind."

With diminishing steam pressure, speed was again reduced—to 20 knots.

Gunnery officer O'Donnell noticed off the port bow that "one dive-bomber caught fire rather spectacularly. It was believed that it would hit the flight deck. I climbed down into the battle lookout station so I could report where it hit.

"It had disappeared when I got there. One other dive-bomber and two torpedo planes were seen by me to be shot down on the port side. I saw two dive-bombers pass over the ship streaming gasoline from their wings near the fuselage."

Radioman Harold Littlefield, thankful that he had escaped any hurt on his high, open perch, noticed "a quick burning sensation in my arm and I looked down. I saw a little cut under my arm between my elbow and my shoulder.

"Seeing that it was just a slight cut and not an artery, I let 'er bleed. It didn't hurt anyway. I don't know just what it was that hit me, but imagined that it must have been a piece of shrapnel.

"Another fellow up there with me got hit in just about the same way I did. It was nothing at all."

Others, too, experienced no more serious injuries than did Littlefield or his companion.

A pharmacist's mate, in charge of the after battle-dressing station, had encountered some difficulty because the overhead light had been broken by vibrations either from hits or the carrier's own guns.

98

". . . One patient reported to this station because he had torn the nail of his left index finger approximately half off while handling 5-inch ammunition. The nail was removed, finger bandaged and patient returned to duty.

"One ambulatory patient suffering from heat exhaustion was brought to this station from the nearby after steering gear room. He was treated, observed and returned to duty in about one-half hour.

"Drinking water originally provided for personnel in this area was inadequate. The temperature and humidity were high as all ventilation had been off for nearly four hours. Water jugs were empty and many men came to this station asking for a drink. To avoid all possible heat exhaustion, several water jugs were filled and much drinking water dispensed as ueeded from our large reserve supply (twelve gallons in wooden kegs and thirty gallons in an overhead emergency steel tank.)"

Tom Nixon, in central control, found that subsequent torpedo hits had jolted the ship not quite so "comfortably" as the first. "Violent, terrific vibrations broke several light globes and made the bulkheads quiver."

His efforts, now, involved trying to make the inclinometer swing back to dead center. He and others in this compartment were "instructing wing tank control to commence pumping water and oil to the high [starboard] side, then checking charts of tanks full and empty and tonnage—figuring therefrom how long it would take to get the ship on an even keel."

Tom heard the captain's voice asking for "this estimate," which he gave. When the young officer double-checked his mental rule of thumb, "the figures came so close to the estimate that I decided not to send the captain a revise."

On his battle telephones he ordered repair parties to the badly hurt forward 5-inch gun gallery where there had been such carnage, then looked over the pins, pegs and chalk marks on the damage chart, the pattern of which changed from second to second as calls crackled in.

"Pop" Healy entered after a personal inspection of the worst hit areas and asked if the repair parties were dispatched. Then the damage control officer double-checked the estimate Tom Nixon had already sent to the captain.

Healy, who appeared to Nixon to be "calm as always," shook his head and said his own calculations on the degree and extent of damage "differ somewhat." In almost the same breath he added that the discrepancies were not "sufficient" to bother the *Lexington*'s commanding officer.

He then called the bridge to report "bulkheads holding," and that all would be "shipshape soon."

Commissary men at this point carried in sandwiches, apples and coffee. The food proved a stimulant to the men, who soon were swept by self-assurance, "smug and confident that they would soon have the ship back on even keel," as Nixon would recall.

"Our previous drills with wing tank control for counterflooding," he noted, "were now proving themselves to have been sound."

. . . The last of the Japanese dive bombers roared by. The pilot pressed his machine gun trigger as if in a final, spiteful fillip. His bomb missed, close by. Flak bursts from the task force trailed the plane until it was out of sight.

At 1132, Duckworth recorded, "one of our SBD's tried to approach the ship and was shot down by cruiser and destroyer fire. At least he landed in the water and apparently under partial control while they were firing.

"No one could stop the fire in time."

Angry and frantic at once, Dudley "with no time to look up the signal hoist from the signal book that friendly aircraft were approaching, I ordered the flag hoist *Negat Roger*, meaning 'cease fire with main battery!' "

Another SBD droned in amidst a peppering of small-caliber shells, then the barrage seemed to dwindle. Dudley figured the hoist had "seemed to work."

Duckworth continued: "We were about 120° out of the wind and turning hard right with about 20 knots. The landing signal officer [with his two large hand paddles] waved him off but to no avail. He struck the deck in a wild diving turn, caught and broke number 2 wire and finally went over the side just aft of the barrier, taking part of an arresting gear with him."

The *Morris* was able to rescue both pilot and radioman gunner. Now, the air officer could finish his entry: ". . .The attack was completed."

It was just two minutes after seven bells, in the Coral Sea. A smell of burned explosives, hot metal, smoldering paint, cork and various insulating material hung as miasma and immediate memory over the sweltering ship.

The *Lexington* was bruised, bloodied and staggering. Yet, she was still afloat, and in the fight.

11

"Steaming as before . . ."

"Suddenly," it was apparent to Captain Sherman, "all was quiet again.

"It was as though some hidden director had signaled for silence. The Japanese planes were no longer in sight, the guns had stopped shooting for lack of targets. The sea was still dotted with burning planes; our own aircraft were seen in the distance, assembling to be ready for further action. But the enemy were through.

"I looked at my watch. The entire attack had lasted just nine minutes. It seemed hours since we had first sighted the enemy planes."

Word was passed over the speaker system, which had functioned remarkably, that the attack was over.

As though he, too, had heard and understood, Wags crawled out from under his master's bed in the emergency quarters next to the bridge. He had been tethered on a long leash, allowing the elderly cocker to poke his nose into the chartroom during short lulls in the attack.

Lieutenant Durant, now acting as the supply officer following the death of Gilmore, ordered resumption of food service as normally as possible. The supply corps, which he believed had sustained thirty casualties, including the death of two officers, had suffered disproportionately.

Frank Binder, from Houston, a first-class buglemaster, was one of the several of his unique rate doubling as quartermaster. (He had served on the bridge by the phones during the action.) Now he walked below to answer the half-hearted call for "chow," aware of a "great unreality" of time and place.

When Binder reached his compartment, which was also his eating hall, he lost his appetite, then felt sick—"all the smell of burned flesh."

Olliff's "show" was over, but he remained somewhat concerned over possible delayed-action bombs. He quit the photo lab to resume working on his aircraft's cranky fuel pump.

Now he encountered new troubles: The bombs and torpedoes had loosened the spider's web of fuel line connections. There apparently were leaks all over the big Pratt and Whitney radial.

Len Olliff wondered if he would *ever* get that shower. He was so hot, sweaty and greasy. . . .

At least there was new illumination now from small holes pocking the sides of the hangar deck. These were caused by shrapnel from nearby bomb hits in the water.

Wood, the radioman, was not so scared anymore. He returned to the radio shack topside.

The speed, at 1142, was slowed to 17 knots, pending efforts to increase the pressure on remaining boilers to spin the turbine generators.

On the *New Orleans*, Chaplain Forgy perceived "the firing ended abruptly. . . .

"A corpsman bracing himself against a cot looked hopefully toward Busby and asked the question that was on every tongue in the room. 'Did we get hit? We've been in this list an awfully long time. Feels like we're taking water.'

104

"Busby inverted the palms of his hand in a resigned I-don't-know gesture.

"Belowdecks we had no way of knowing that the task force was swinging about in a wide turn and that the bomb that lifted the *No-Boat* had not touched us. It was a near miss that exploded in the sea about a hundred feet off our fantail and sent a tidal wave of water cascading over the aft end of the ship.

"I resolved to see if I could arrange to change my battle station to topside in future battles and send word of what was happening down to these men who were starving for information below. I figured I would be more useful doing this than merely lying flat on the deck down in sick bay.

"The welcome notes of *Secure* rang through the speaker, terminating the GQ.

"Dr. Evans and I hurried up the ladders to the quarterdeck. About 2,000 yards off our port bow was the *Lexington*. I felt reassured when I saw her. She was still the gallant lady of the sea, racing through the water. A wisp of smoke was coming through her decks, but it did not appear that she had a bad fire aboard. I was sure she was going to be all right after all.

"However, men on the deck told us she had taken at least one direct bomb hit and from three to five torpedoes. It was hard to believe as I watched her cutting through the water with her long-familiar majestic bearing. The *Lex* can take anything, I thought, if three torpedoes and a bomb don't bother her anymore than that."

Many of those serving in the task force contemplated the carrier with much the same compassion they would accord a parent who had survived major surgery. And like Chaplain Forgy, serious doubts as to ultimate recovery simply did not occur.

"We had a lot of work to do around the battery," Lieutenant Williams wrote. "We had some mess attendants who were supposed to be ammunition bearers, but they had enough ammunition right there at the guns so they didn't have anything to do. They were pretty well scared, back against the bulkhead there not having anything to occupy their minds.

"We broke into some quarters, got some blankets, some brooms and tried to push the water and oil off to where it would drain out of the battery. I found plenty to do in getting the battery cleared up. There were an awful lot of empty shell casings to push out of the way.

"One mess attendant, I remember putting a broom in his hand. He just stood there. He couldn't move. So I worked his arms a few times and got him going. So he kept going.

"There was another one of those little mess attendants who was one of the finest boys I'd ever seen. He was scared plenty, too, like all of us, but I never saw anybody turn to and work better than he did. All did pretty well as soon as they had something to do.

"We got the battery cleared away, but some gasoline was spraying on us from where a bomb had loosened that hose."

The ship was imperceptibly settling. As she did so, water was pushing up the gasoline to the top of the tanks.

Lieutenant Coward, who had lost two officers in sky aft including Max Price and several enlisted men, was working on a philosophy of personal distraction, much like Williams'. There was a lot to "swab," especially so since it was apparent that the bomb that had caused the casualties had also partially detonated a ready box of shells.

Incandescent heat and blast effect had left men blackened, "frozen dead at their guns," like the people of Pompeii caught in Vesuvius' lava flow.

Even if there had not been a practical reason for "cleaning up," the recent Naval Academy graduate still was determined to maintain morale. He thought the carrier herself "looked in pretty good shape, aside from the torpedo holes." After all, she probably had taken only three of the twelve torpedoes the ordnance expert in Pearl Harbor estimated she could "swallow."

"Mort" Seligman, the executive officer, remained a study in activity, moving throughout the carrier as he had been doing during the attack. He found that ". . . Commander

106

Gilmore and Commander Trojakowski were probably killed in the passageway by the blast of the first bomb or possibly by exploding 5-inch ammunition. It was evident that some personnel in the coding room on the starboard side suffered severely from the effects of this blast.

"There was another fire in the forward starboard Marine compartment and one near the incinerator, in the same vicinity. I proceeded there as soon as possible. The fire in the Marine area had been localized and was not dangerous. No sign of fire was then observed near the incinerator.

"A bomb had struck near the gig boat pocket on the port side, with severe effects on personnel. The fire was, however, quickly and effectively handled."

Since it seemed to Seligman that most of the fires were now "in control," he went off in search of "Pop" Healy to obtain the damage-control officer's assessment of the situation.

Somewhere between the captain's motorboat and the 5-inch forward port gun, Joe Hart had joined a random group of firefighters. He had brushed off most of the dry foamite chemical and now, like his companions, was trying to coax enough water pressure so that he could make headway against the flames, crackling ominously around the ready boxes of ammunition.

After watching the water "come and go" desultorily for a few minutes, Joe decided he'd visit his locker and put on some clean clothes. As he started to do so, he glanced involuntarily at the stack, where his brother had been on the .50-caliber guns.

They were now lowering the wounded, and the dead. He saw an officer, coming down in a sling, terribly mangled. The machinist mate from Macon walked over to where another group of men was receiving these casualties and asked one of them if Tom was "okay." One of them looked at him "kind of funny"; another shrugged.

Joe did not tarry long. He continued toward his locker.

The ship's company was being organized into rescue and repair parties. In one was Ensign Cecil E. "Pat" Dowling, a Canadian who had been naturalized after World War I

service in the United States Navy. A bos'n until 1941, sometimes scourge of green ensigns, Dowling was among the experienced officers in the *Lexington*'s construction and repair
department.

As a member of Repair Party 1, Dowling "received several orders in quick succession to investigate fires and assist
with wounded in different localities. One was the coding
room, others the executive officer's stateroom, sky forward,
sky aft, gig boat pocket (amidships) and the wardroom.

"After all inspections were made and wounded taken
care of, the damage-control officer in central station was
notified.

"Central station then reported to all repair parties that
the ship was on an even keel and making about 25 knots
and that all damage was under control.

"I was then ordered by the damage-control officer to take
a look over the port side of the ship and try and locate the
frame numbers where the torpedoes had entered. I had located one torpedo hit at about frame 90 in wake of the gig
boat pocket. The blister at that point was torn loose, the
20-mm. guns had been thrown back into the pocket and
all life nets in the vicinity were torn loose and hanging."

If the repair officers and repair parties were extremely
busy, the doctors were possibly even more so.

"The casuals" were streaming into all dressing stations. Dr.
White reported: "Their injuries consisted of first- and second-
degree burns, shrapnel wounds, contusions and lacerated
wounds, blast injuries and simple and compound fractures.
A number of injured had received first aid at outlying stations,
consisting of application of tourniquets where indicated, tannic
acid jelly to burns and morphine where indicated.

"The injured arrived in such great numbers that the dressing station became congested, so flash clothing, dungarees
and skivvies were cut off and a quick survey of the extent of
the injuries was made.

"Those men who did not show critical injury were carried
or walked into the division sleeping spaces immediately out-

board of the dressing station, where they were bunked and received further medical attention as time would allow.

"One PhM1c [pharmacist's mate 1st class] was detailed to these spaces and carried out such orders given by the medical officer, reapplication of tourniquets on patients with arterial bleeding every twenty minutes, dressing burns that covered large areas of the body with sterile gauze for protection, and general nursing care.

"First- and second-degree burned patients became chilled very easily and asked for great quantities of water to drink. Blankets were plentiful and were used on every patient, as nearly all showed some degree of shock.

"Patients who had extensive burns and those with considderable blood loss from shrapnel wounds were given a unit of blood plasma. An estimate of nine patients died, all of whom were in a moribund condition on arrival at the dressing station. Causes of death in six cases were large shrapnel wounds of the abdomen and chest. Two patients apparently died as a result of a blast. An examination showed no external wounds except for superficial powder burns of the face. Both had been unconscious, pulse thready and respiration very shallow and irregular.

"Contact was made by ship's service phone with the main station, sick bay. A report of conditions in the aviation battle-dressing station was made. Supplies were plentiful and requests for dressings, morphine, and tannic acid jelly for first-aid men on the flight deck and main deck were filled."

[No damage was sustained in main battle-dressing station. There were twelve patients in the ward, one of whom was considered a stretcher case—appendectomy, in his third postoperative day, in good condition.]

"Inspection by a repair party showed that the sick bay country and storeroom on the deck below were undamaged. Casuals began to arrive very soon after the cessation of firing as follows:

" 'Lacerated wound anterior surface right ankle. Sulfathiazole powder used, wound sutured and returned to ward.'

109

" 'Extensive second-degree burn of face and body. Clothing blown off by blast. Morphine, tannic acid jelly and spray, blood plasma, and to bed.'

" 'Extensive second-degree burn of face and hands, some trunk and leg involvement. Morphine, tannic acid jelly and spray, blood plasma 250 cc, to bed.'

"A report from the main deck, forward collecting station revealed heavy damage in that vicinity, with the death of Commander W. C. Trojakowski. Two corpsmen and needed fresh supplies were despatched from main battle-dressing station, and a new station was established in the captain's cabin, which functioned in an excellent manner. It was learned that the battle-dressing locker at this station had been demolished with the blast from the ammunition lockers.

"Aviation battle-dressing station reported at this time that many casuals were arriving, with injuries consisting of burns of varying degrees and shrapnel wounds of varying type. Supplies were plentiful and work was progressing satisfactorily.

"After battle-dressing station reported a few casuals by telephone. Work was progressing satisfactorily and the station was undamaged."

As Radioman Littlefield noted, "everything seemed okay and we were sure that we were going to bring our wounded ship home with very little trouble. We were making excellent speed. We already had taken the list out of her, our flight deck was okay and we were taking our own planes on."

All in all, "taking stock on the *Lexington*," Sherman decided, "things were not so bad as they might have been. The small fires down below were being fought by the damage-control parties, who reported that they would soon have them under control. No smoke from the flames was showing abovedecks. The ship had taken only a 7° list from the torpedo hits, and this was rapidly being corrected by shifting water ballast.

110

"The engine room reported full power and speed available if I wanted it. Our flight deck was intact. We felt like throwing out our chests at our condition after the attack."

By 1153, Dudley logged, "all fires on flight deck out. Steadied on course 130° (T)." Three minutes later, "turning left, steadied on course 028° (T). Report from after signal station of casualties nearby: 1 killed, 3 seriously injured, 5 injured. Repair parties inspecting and repairing damage."

Although "both elevators were out of commission and in up position," the *Lexington* at twelve o'clock high noon was at 20 knots, "steaming as before."

12

"Bremerton here we come!"

At 1223 "Red" Gill reported that the carrier was hitting 25 knots, "without trouble."

In the navigator's book Dudley continued, "List all removed from the ship by shifting fluids. 1230, opened vents necessary for ventilating and turned into wind."

Proud that the damage-control organization was "functioning smoothly," the executive officer decided there was "no apparent cause for concern." He then "determined to visit the dressing stations and sick bay to obtain an idea of the number and condition of casualties."

There, and at all first-aid areas, the wounded were continuing to arrive. At one of them, the after aviation "collecting" station, Lieutenant A. T. "Al" Smith, of the Dental Corps, pinch-hitting for the MD's, reported: "A Marine sergeant was the first wounded man to enter the compartment from Battery Four. He had multiple gunshot wounds from a strafing plane, which seemed to be made from small-caliber bullets.

"A few seconds later two more Marines entered with bullet wounds. One patient had a wound of the lower leg and the other patient a bullet wound in the back of the shoulder over the area of the scapula.

"All patients were laid on the deck and made comfortable. The wounds were bandaged by the hospital corpsman and myself, hemorrhages arrested and morphine given. Patients were then covered with blankets.

"I was called into the adjoining compartment to look at a Marine who had been brought in with a bullet wound in the region of the heart. His was the only death so far at this first-aid station.

"Shortly, three more patients arrived with multiple bullet wounds. These were taken care of and treated in the same manner. Two had bones in the forearm splintered. Then two more arrived, with burns on the arms. Tannic acid jelly was applied."

The "patient" ship was responding to treatment, too. Within the past hour, the flooded firerooms 2, 4 and 6 had been pumped dry. The list, which had been estimated variously from 6° to 12° to port, had been removed by shifting fuel from port to the "high" starboard tanks.

Central control, in fact, had performed such a skillful rebalancing of the task force's Goliath that Lieutenant Williams was prepared to swear that she had ended up with a 1° opposite list, to starboard. Had the list not been compensated, he rationalized, the planes ultimately would have had to cease being landed. In enemy waters it was a case of "landing or losing" the carrier's aircraft.

"The best estimate of the situation," noted Junker, the engineering officer, in further appraisal, "appears to be that the outboard bulkhead in the lower space—gasoline pump room—was damaged and leaking slightly, and that the outboard bulkhead in the upper space—gas control room—was undamaged.

"It seems definitely established that gasoline cleavage gauges and other gas fittings in the upper space were not damaged. Following inspection, the lower space—gas pump room—was flooded with salt water and the upper space—gas control room—was filled with CO_2 [carbon dioxide].

"Approximately twenty-five persons were stationed in the I.C. [interior communications] room, central station and forward distribution room area and did not report presence of gasoline fumes. The deck in these places was undamaged.

"The only space below the first platform deck which is known to have been inspected was the evaporator room, where the port outboard bulkhead between it and the elevator bottle well was noted to be bulged inboard.

"Oil was noted on the deck of the general workshop issuing room and adjacent passageway outboard on the third deck. The oil undoubtedly came from a ruptured fuel oil filling line which passes through both spaces.

"It was reported but not confirmed that one torpedo detonated forward on the port side just abaft the stem. No inspection of this area was made to confirm an explosion having occurred. An additional torpedo was reported to have hit the ship while traveling on a converging course, but this torpedo did not detonate."

All the while, Duckworth was working at flank speed getting his flight deck and department back to some state approximating normal: ". . . bomb-hit hole was no longer smoking, so we washed down the flight deck in vicinity to clear the chemical extinguisher mess.

"Both elevators were reported to be permanently out of commission because of torpedo damage to the hydraulic machinery located below the forward elevator well. About the same time I sent aft for a report on the gasoline system [and found] the port side out of commission.

"We were turning into the wind from a northerly heading. Very shortly thereafter we landed on board four VF combat patrol and nine SBD's. Three of these were from the morning search, the rest from the antitorpedo plane patrol.

"While these planes were being respotted for takeoff, I reported to the captain the condition of the gasoline system

and that I was not refueling until I was certain all fires were out. We planned to delay until just before the attack group returned. I also reported the condition of the elevators and explained that we would have to throw some planes over the side to make room for the rest.

"Two of the SBD's on deck were badly shot up, so the propellers and loose equipment were removed for spares and the planes pushed over the ramp.

"The log shows a report of all fires out at 1233 [and] we commenced refueling the planes on deck. The fighters were completed first and were launched."

From the *Phelps,* Beck perceived, with admiration, that the *Lex*'s "gallant crew had extinguished all fires (we thought), corrected list and trim, and she was again steaming in fleet formation at 25 knots! All was well, or so we hoped. . . ."

At 1241 "Red" Gill, the fighter director, recorded "friendly planes bearing 280° distance 36 miles. These planes were reported friendly from the time they appeared on the screen, but in spite of that they were fired upon when they came within gun range."

Exactly one minute later, at 1242, "Heine" Junker was given a report that was at once disquieting and not wholly anticipated: "Fumes of considerable intensity in the general workshop and in the CPO [chief petty officer] messing spaces."

The engineer officer ordered "all personnel . . . immediately to evacuate these areas."

Near Tom Nixon in central station, Donald Albrightson, a chief yeoman from Sunnyvale, California, was thinking, as had "Red" Coward, "Bremerton here we come!" A genial and particularly efficient noncommissioned officer, Albrightson was in charge of officers' records and assignments.

While pegging or pinning onto the diagrammatic board of the *Lexington* the locations where torpedoes or bombs had hit and fires had been or might still be smoldering, Albrightson had to admit that "the furthest thing" from his mind was the chance that "the lady could be sunk."

Ed Muhlenfeld, well removed and above Albrightson's position, was nonetheless experiencing similar flashes: "We've gotten through this and, oh boy, we're going home!"

Not then aware of Junker's knowledge of the fumes, Sherman wrote: "We proceeded to land our planes which were in the vicinity and out of ammunition or gas after their air battles. We replenished the ammunition of our guns and refilled the ammunition hoists to be ready for another attack should one come.

"Lieutenant Commander 'Pop' Healy, down in central station below the armored deck, phoned the bridge to inform me that all damage was under control."

Nixon heard "Pop" conclude, "All torpedo damage shored up and all fires out."

Nixon looked at the draft indicator to check on how deep the carrier was in the water, and at the inclinometer to see if she were on even keel. He felt "smug" every time a degree of list was taken off. He timed the period of roll with a stopwatch and noted it had not approached danger point.

Then, without warning, Nixon was aware of "a terrific explosion and a sheet of flame, a sense of horror. . . .!"

To Albrightson, the sensation was one of "molten lava pouring over me, then nothing."

In the adjoining distribution room, Lieutenant Williamson, the electrical officer, saw "a bright red flash" even as he was slammed into the switchboard.

"A gale of wind with the force of a hurricane blew through the door from central station and pinned me to the board," he would report. "The wind seemed to be made of streams of flame and myriads of sparks.

"The gale lasted for only a few seconds and left nothing but heavy, choking fumes."

PART 2

DOWN TO ETERNITY

13

"I'm all right, padre."

At 12:47, according to the captain's watch, "the *Lexington* was suddenly shaken by a terrific internal explosion which seemed to come from the bottom of the ship."

It then "rocked the huge structure more violently than had anything we had received during the battle. Smoke began emerging from around the edges of the elevator on the flight deck [and also, as Dudley perceived, from the forward bomb elevator, adjacent to the plane elevator]."

"We called central station but found the connection broken. The rudder indicator on the bridge was also out. All telephones were dead except a sound-powered one to the engine room. However, reports of huge fires breaking out in the vicinity of central station were soon received."

"The station itself was an inferno."

Dr. White was just finishing his "after-action report" to the effect that he could not reach the engineer's battle-dressing station when he was abruptly thrown from his desk. He dictated later:

121

"A terrific blast sustained in main sick bay country followed by much smoke and gas, but no fire. Carried through the air for a distance of ten to fifteen feet and landed me in a sitting position."

He also watched the bizarre spectacle of "other personnel in the sick bay country carried varying short distances."

Seligman was "blown like a cork out of a bottle," by Captain Sherman's phraseology, as he was entering the hatch leading to the sick bay forward.

"I was not injured," Seligman thought, even though actually an ankle had been sprained. "I proceeded aft on the second deck to endeavor to locate the source of the explosion. A severe fire was burning in the CPO passageway and at other points in the officer area. It was especially severe near the gunnery office, but there was no indication of fire below the second deck."

Williamson regained consciousness to find that he was lying quite alone amidst the shattered gauges and controls of the electrical board and in a "nest" of fragmented glass. Flash burns had seared his entire back, in some areas down to his spine and muscles. He struggled up and opened the door, which had slammed shut again, "for air."

He passed through thick smoke coming from the hatchway to central station, not more than fifteen feet from his switchboard. He located "Heine" Junker in Number 2 boiler passageway and informed him that "hydrogen gas in the forward storage battery area had blown up" and that as well there were "many injured in central station and interior communications."

Many of the carrier's vital controls and communications had ceased to function. Among these were the engine telegraph on the bridge, for relaying orders mechanically to the engineers; the rudder angle indicator; and the Walker Log, an electrical device connected to a small propeller to record mileage. Various phone circuits were dead, necessitating the use of the relatively inefficient sound-powered telephones.

The forward gyro compass, one of two, also had become inoperative.

A furious explosion seals the fate of the *Lexington*.

Frustrated that he could not reach central station, "Pat" Dowling kept trying the secondary circuits to "call up" Healy. He tried switching headsets, thinking the concussions might have broken some. All was silence, at best static.

"Raging fires," Sherman wrote, "fed by gasoline, broke out from ruptured vents and risers [vertical pipes coming off a water or fire main]. The water main was broken in the area of the explosion, making work of combating the flames extremely difficult. Long hoses had to be led from aft and only low water pressure could be maintained.

"But we expected to save the carrier."

Dr. White, feeling himself over, realized that he had "sustained fracture of his right shoulder, contusions and lacerations of left ankle and contusions of right ankle."

He noted with surprise that others, even though they had been knocked down by the explosion, apparently had not been hurt at all. Satisfied for the moment that there were "no new injured personnel" for which he could not account, the chief surgeon ordered "main sick bay country" moved to the upper deck.

Fred Hartson had locked the brakes of his plane when he felt the blast. He ran for cover. Just as quickly he realized the *Lexington* was not under attack.

Joe Hart, from Macon, never reached his locker, to which he had been heading with interruptions. He discovered the passageways filled with smoke. Men, holding arms over their eyes, coughed past him. Some were assisted by rescuers.

Hart started back for the flight deck.

Ensign Muhlenfeld went below for the "head." Clouds of smoke were issuing from each of several he approached.

"To hell with it," he would remember thinking, although dispassionately enough. He turned about and never thought of the "head" again.

"Heine" Junker "personally checked the forward storage battery supply vent in number 2 boiler intake," where he discovered "a heavy brown oil smoke coming from this intake which hinted that there was an oil fire in the vicinity of the battery locker or that acid-resisting paint in the battery locker was smoldering."

The chief engineer "believed that this explosion was caused by gasoline fumes leaking into the motor generator compartment and being set off probably from brush sparking of one of the motor generators or some other electrical sparking."

Chief Binder, the buglemaster, had a hunch that sulphuric acid fumes had something to do with the blast. Others placed the center farther forward.

Whatever the origin or location, Junker knew there was no time to lose. He ordered an assistant, Lieutenant Frederick W. Hawes, commanding "A" Division, to get down to "the scene of the explosion." This was a broad and as yet imperfectly defined area affecting many of the ship's compartments closed prior to the attack, and extending through a midships section comprising central station, the forward gyro,

124

electrical board and interior communications compartments down to certain firerooms.

The engineering officer wished to know not only all of the boundaries of this blackened no-man's-land but, more important, if any remained alive within.

"Freddie" Hawes, now exhorting Repair Party 4 to "fall in" with utmost haste, was reserved of nature, a tallish, blond officer from Centralia, Washington. He had graduated from Annapolis in 1934 where, as Sherman before him, he had excelled as a boxer. Aboard the *Lexington,* Hawes had proven himself a meticulous, conscientious leader far beyond the call to "regs."

Lieutenant Hawes, so at least "Red" Coward thought, could move through a ship "blindfolded." He popped up at any and all hours of the night in unlikely places, flashlight in hand. He maintained "ninety-one files on everything," knew "every valve and bolt" in his own division "country."

A stickler for detail, there were those who would attest that Hawes sometimes measured crewmen's hair to make certain that it was not longer than the regulation two inches, with a safe margin of several millimeters. "Freddie," however, commanded respect not only because of a manifest knowledge of his duties but because he was the sort who refused to issue an order that he could not personally carry out. He much preferred to "go it alone" were there the least show of reluctance to accompany him.

There was no reluctance this afternoon in Repair 4, heading down to the damaged forward areas below the hangar deck, especially on the starboard side. Among this unit was Erich Eger, 18, an electrician third class, one of a small group of friends from the Milwaukee area who had been offered a tour of duty on the carrier in 1940 while with the Naval Reserve. Erich also played trumpet in the ship's band.

Wearing a gas mask, the slender Erich, attached to a safety rope, squirmed through a scuttle to the forward generator room. This was connected both to the gyro room and the forward distribution board—dark, smoky wastelands that had borne the full fury of the explosion. Others in the repair group followed. The men groped ahead, not knowing what they would find or if even the deck plates were still below the blanketing of smoke. Eger heard the generators "still whirring in spite of their punishment. This sound in itself renewed his faith that "this ship is going to stay here." He did not believe she would sink.

Nonetheless, there was very little real solace in the generator area. Probing behind the faint illumination of just one battle lantern, he could see the "glow coming through the bulkheads" and knew the fires were far from controlled. For that matter, this was the first proof that flames actually existed in explosion "country."

It seemed to Eger, as he progressed, that the carrier was one endless maze of ladders and damaged compartments. He also was thankful for Hawes's diagrammatic knowledge of the ship's interior.

Soon, "Willie" Williamson, the electrical officer, who had recovered sufficiently to join the search, heard someone call, "Take it easy!"

Thus, Repair 4 found the first explosion victim, lying in a passageway half awash in a slimy mixture of six inches of oil and water. The man was picked up, carried to a hatch in the generator room and hauled topside through a recessed elevator well. Then he was moved aft by stretcher.

One by one, Repair 4 rescued approximately twenty people. Hawes,* who had worn only a gas mask, so that his men

---

* For commanding this rescue party, Hawes received the Navy Cross, the only one to be awarded aboard the carrier this day. The citation read:

"For extraordinary heroism and distinguished service in the line of his profession as officer-in-charge of Repair Party #4 of the USS *Lexington* in action against Japanese forces in the Coral Sea on May 7 and 8, 1942. He led his repair party into gas-filled compartments, in which there were frequent explosions, in order to effect the rescue of wounded officers and men. With complete disregard for his own safety, he personally led rescue parties into dangerous areas, twice losing consciousness, and both times returning to lead his men. By his courageous leadership he effected the rescue of at least 20 of the wounded. His conduct and devotion to duty on this occasion were in keeping with the best traditions of the naval service.

might have the scarce oxygen masks, then moved to the starboard compartments next to the hangar deck, "where there was light from opened portholes." He sat beside Eger for "a chance for rest and fresh air."

Williamson, who believed the heat in the compartments was upwards of 150 degrees Fahrenheit, heard Hawes say, "It's no use trying anymore." He added that about all they could hope to accomplish now was to identify the bodies of those past saving.

As Junker observed of the results of Repair 4's efforts, "this rescue work was carried on under most difficult conditions." The engineer officer had been provided with two important pieces of intelligence: that there *were* fires forward and that oil and water lay upon some passageways.

Now even the slowest witted could deduce that the *Lexington* was leaking. And if she *were* taking water, her hull had been torn and weakened.

"Heine" Junker next gave orders to shore up what forward bulkheads could be reached.

Tom Nixon and Albrightson were the only apparent survivors of central station. Tom was dazed, his clothes scorched and shredded when he was seen standing on deck by a classmate, Lieutenant J. E. "Ed" Pace, of Admiral Fitch's staff. Ed at once remembered what Tom had scribbled in his *Lucky Bag,* the Annapolis yearbook, at graduation:

"When the *Lexington* goes down in the next war we'll be darn glad to have you on the sister ship. I'll fix it with the skipper."

Pace had just been assigned to the *Lexington* at the time of this curious if chance prophecy and Nixon to the *Saratoga.* Subsequent events were to bring them together again on Captain Sherman's carrier.

"Pop" Healy, the brains and strong man of central station, was not to be found. As further testimony to the blind waste of war, Quartermaster Thomas K. Bult, "one of the most alert" of his rate, by Dudley's estimation, had been sent to Healy's post as a "relatively secure belowdecks point."

The captain wanted Bult saved even if the whole bridge and

the staff were wiped out. Now Bult along with Healy was gone.

Dr. Roach, who at first had thought that a "sleeper" or de-layed-action bomb had caused the detonation, was sum-moned to the hangar deck from engineer's battle-dressing station.

"Taking one corpsman with me," he wrote, "I proceeded to the hangar area." It was not easy getting there. He found "some of the compartments had been struck and either wholly or partially flooded with oil or water so that we were forced to take a rather circuitous route and finally arrived at the hangar deck. We found this area to be in semidarkness and filled with smoke.

"On the hangar deck there were a good many people from the repair parties and we were immediately told that there had been an explosion and a fire down in central station. Men were being brought up to the deck. Some of them had already perished ["mummies," Fred Hartson had thought; like "burned cigars" or "charcoal," others noted in equal horror], some were in a severe state of shock. Some were breathing, some were not, and still others were only injured in a rather minor way.

"In all, approximately twenty-five were brought out and laid on the forward end of the hangar deck just aft of the elevator. All had been burned on the exposed parts of the body, the burns complicated by the effects of the noxious gases, apparently carbon monoxide or some of the nitrous fumes.

"Treatment consisted of artificial respiration, morphine sulfate and tannic acid jelly to the burned areas."

In less than one-quarter of an hour, the smoke became so thick that "it was necessary to wear gas masks," Dr. Roach continued. "The dead and wounded were carried to the after end where the air was better and treatment could be con-tinued. A careful search was made to assure that no one was left behind."

128

This removal, it was apparent to the executive officer, was accomplished "with utter disregard" for Dr. Roach's "own safety."

Aside from the continuing problem of where to place casualties, the major concern, according to Duckworth, the air officer, was the "making of sensible evaluations of changing conditions. It was hard to find out anything after central control was gone."

"One could not obtain the full picture," in the opinion of "Rip" Raring, the aerologist. "We'd pick up little bits of information here and there."

As Jerry O'Donnell, the gunnery officer, sized up the situation, "now we have to make do on our own initiative."

Fires were burning in the chief petty officers' mess and bunk room, one deck above and slightly forward of central station. At first the flames were combated by running a hose down the dumbwaiter shaft to the adjacent food distribution room. The blaze in the admiral's cabin, which had been wrestled almost to a halt, frustratingly flared anew. It was almost a willful thing.

Doors along the second deck passageway were blown open all the distance to sick bay, with "blast effect" extending as far forward as the doctor's office. Other offices were wrecked or set aflame, with damage transcending that merely to a living space and its furniture.

Lieutenant Williams was certain that the explosion had "limited any possibility" of recovering the money from his pay office, where he estimated more than $300,000 "in cash" was locked in two safes.

Meanwhile, rescues and rescue efforts continued. Aviation Chief Ordnanceman Turlington, trying to penetrate to the machine shop in the lower deck, found that the flames had "spread through the supply and disbursing offices instantaneously. Heat became so intense and fumes so dense that they [those men in the immediate compartments] experienced great difficulty in escaping with their lives."

Turlington owed his life on his next trip below to the great strength of a recently promoted warrant gunner, John Sawula, whose pastime was weightlifting. He had already demonstrated that he could lift or open jammed hatches—thick steel doors or lids—as though they were pie plates.

The main force of the initial explosion, according to Sawula, "seemed to be a few feet from us, as if a bomb had come through from the topside. Actually, the explosion was on the deck below. The lights went out immediately throughout; there was a violent hiss, sparks were flying around with a very rapid motion.

"In a very short interval of time the spaces were filled with dense smoke, a red glow came from the bulkheads and the spaces were unbearably hot. We stumbled forward only to find conditions much worse; we then returned to the after end of the passageway and with great difficulty opened the port door, closing the door behind us.

"The smoke was everywhere, and the heat was gradually building up in other compartments. We passed through the band room and made our way to the bomb elevator. The 100-pound bombs were still intact in the band room. From the band room looking across the bomb elevator shaft we could see a fire burning on the other side of the bulkheads by means of small holes in the bulkheads.

"We climbed the shaft, discovered the elevator had been blown into the hatch and the elevator cable was parted. We then climbed back down to the motor room level and started through when a violent gust of smoke and sparks came from below. The bottom of the elevator well throughout our stay there was being filled with water coming from the machine shop.

"We finally made it to the topside."

Carpenter Harry F. Nowack, also investigating, estimated that the "entire wardroom deck was raised about six inches." In Nowack's picked team of five "volunteers"—comprising "you, you, you, you and you"—was Fireman First Class Henry "Hank" Laupan. The husky "Hank," of Russian émigré parentage, was one of the Milwaukee group.

Nowack said he feared that many were trapped in the print shop and sick bay. He led the team down "Indian-file" from the gun deck to the print shop, where 5-inch ammunition was stored.

Laupan was able to assist in the rescue of only one man before he too went faint from smoke. He had to be hauled out for air.

Another of the party, investigating the generators where "Heine" Junker thought sparks might have triggered the blast, slid on the oily film covering the deck as he heard "a sound of rushing air." Becoming alarmed, he wriggled out through a scuttle just in time. He was "shaken" by a "minor explosion" even as he emerged.

It was increasingly perilous for anyone to go below. O'Donnell, who had previously ordered the forward 5-inch magazine flooded, decided to make certain it actually was filled with water. The gunnery officer was especially concerned with his inability to "communicate with the men stationed in the lower handling rooms," the first in the chain of ammunition passers. One, John E. Whitham, a Californian and married, had been in charge of the forward magazines.

Minute by minute, O'Donnell's fears were turning to conviction that "all the men there were lost."

Driven back on his first try by smoke and blackness, the gunnery officer realized he was not sufficiently familiar with the location of auxiliary flood control handles and levers to reach them in the dark.

"I returned topside," O'Donnell reported, "and found two gunner's mates, who had stood integrity watches for some time. We got lights and put on masks and started down the sick bay hatch. At that instant there occurred an explosion which blew us back up the hatch.

"We ran aft along the warrant officers' country passage. On the next hatch aft, a man was sitting on the scuttle against a pressure which had built up below. I believe one of the gunner's mates helped him secure that scuttle."

Meanwhile, Chaplain Markle had located Gunner Whitham, coming up from below "slowly, under his own power

131

but badly burned and in a state of shock." The chaplain continued:

"We helped him to the captain's cabin where we gave him water, a hypodermic and applied tannic acid jelly to his badly burned body. He appeared to be stunned." Down "a long passageway" leading from the cabin, the chaplain passed some forty wounded, lying on stretchers, blankets or just the bare decking.

". . . They'd wave and say, 'I'm all right, padre," or 'Okay, chaplain' or silently wave to convey that meaning. They seemed to gain comfort by having someone come by. Although many were badly burned and wounded, they were all quite calm.

"They seemed to know me and appreciated a word of interest and encouragement."

Now Markle turned his attention to new groups of wounded, those being evacuated from main sick bay. Some walked, including a day-old appendectomy patient; others had to be passed up through scuttles "barely large enough for a man to squeeze through."

It appeared that a state of disaster at sea had—for the moment at least—been satisfactorily "organized."

14

"We got a 1,000-pound hit!"

Dudley, the navigator, recorded at 1313: "Changed course to 080°. . . . 1317 turned into wind. 1319, another internal explosion felt. Rudder angle indicator and dead-reckoning tracer out of commission."

The carrier, which was steaming almost due east, went dark in virtually all spaces belowdecks.

This second or possibly third internal explosion, half an hour after the first, appeared "less severe" to Seligman. He was wearing a helmet almost jauntily as he raced about the ship at flank speed.

"By this time," he reported, "heat, smoke and gas conditions were so bad as to make it impossible for men not equipped with rescue breathers to enter the [lower] area.

"The small supply of breathers and oxygen bottles available in the ship's allowance was soon exhausted, but the men and officers of the repair parties, augmented by men from the air department and deck divisions, continued to enter the smoke-, flame- and gas-filled compartments only with gas masks, without asbestos suits or fog nozzles.

"The latter were inadequate. Carbon monoxide was undoubtedly present and gas masks were totally ineffective. During this period there were successive minor explosions, some apparently from 5-inch ammunition in the CPO country, others from the vicinity of the original blast.

"The lack of water from the forward hoses was an almost insurmountable handicap, but it is believed that the original fire on the second deck might have been controlled if it had not been for new fires. Meanwhile, it had been discovered that the initial blast had probably occurred somewhere in the vicinity of central station and that the additional detonations in that area had started fires below the armored deck."

Normally, firemain pressure was held at 60 pounds or more per square inch. With all three pump rooms—one forward, one in the engine room, one aft—in operation, the pressure could be boosted to about 80 pounds, sufficient for fighting almost any fire.

The explosion left only number 3 pump, aft, in operation. Although hoses were switched to different "risers," the hydrant-like pipes, only 20 pounds of pressure could be coaxed out of those on the flight deck. Not only was there now only one-third pump capacity, but the cast-iron mains, installed when the *Lexington* was being constructed as a cruiser, had been cracked either by the bombing and torpedoing or the explosions, or both.

However, there was also this consideration: Should the mains somehow be restored to pressure, just how many tons of water could be cascaded into the vitals of a ship without capsizing her?

Captain Sherman, who not long before had felt like "throwing out his chest," conceded that the condition of his carrier was worsening. "Extremely grave" but not "hopeless" was the somewhat similar diagnosis of Mort Seligman. At the same time, he recognized that his own well-being was "considerably weakened" by breathing in so much smoke and being "buffeted about by the concussions."

The captain rationalized that the "insidious accumulation of gasoline vapor" was causing most of the trouble, although he suspected, as did his executive officer, that "5-inch shells overheating and discharging were also contributing to the destruction."

"The fire spread aft," Sherman wrote, "and additional communications were gradually being lost. Minor explosions were recurring at frequent intervals, increasing the fire."

Even so, he retained a certain hopefulness that he would pilot his carrier to port, at least to shoal water. The sturdy vessel with several boiler rooms flooded steamed on a south-southwest course toward Australia, clocking 25 knots, or nearly 30 land miles an hour.

Assuming she could sustain this rate, the venerable *Lexington* should reach the Great Barrier Reef, 450 miles to the west, in about fifteen hours; Brisbane, Australia, in twenty-four hours or, if the ship altered course, New Caledonia, to the southeast, in approximately the same time.

If she came about, the *Lexington* could raise the shoals of Rossel Island, in the Louisiades, less than 200 miles north, in seven hours. But Rossel was deep in enemy waters.

Not far ahead, off the port bow, lay Mellish Reef, inhabited at high tide only by albatross and other sea birds.

O'Donnell, meanwhile, remained undaunted in his desire to check flood valves: "It was decided to try the machine shop from aft. It was believed that the forward magazines must have flooded because of the heat and explosions that had occurred about them without their exploding. In the machine shop, there was a full rearm of bombs.

"I reported to the commander what I had observed and what I considered to be the situation. Then I went to the after end of the hangar deck. The torpedo mezzanine was visited. Chief Torpedo Mate Blanton reported that he had twenty-seven torpedoes with warheads on the mezzanine.

"He was ordered to get them as far aft as possible and to commence sprinkling them.

"It was impossible to dispose of them because the torpedo elevator was jammed in the up position. The after end of the hangar deck was smoky and it was beginning to get rather warm. Two young seaman were met coming aft on

135

the hangar deck. They reported that it was very hot and smoky forward.

"I asked about the machine shop. They answered that they had tried the door and that there was water leaking out of the shop and that they did not attempt to get in. I asked them to show me the door. We had masks and hand lanterns. It was impossible to see in the forward end of the hangar.

"I held onto one of these men as the other led the way. Unfortunately, the man whom I was holding onto got a little too far to the right so that he and I walked off the hangar deck into the elevator well.

"In falling, I lost my mask, but I did not get hurt. However, it was difficult to breathe and impossible to see because of the smoke. The man with the light checked the door, which was still leaking much water. He then led us back along the hangar deck."

Yet, critical as Jerry O'Donnell had found the condition of the *Lexington* to be, he thought there remained no evidence of panic or hysteria on board. Chaplain Markle previously had commented on this.

In fact, even in the engine room, with the fans off, an increasing hot oven of grease and steam, Vernon Highfill held firm in the knowledge that "the big pumps would pump 36,000 gallons a minute." He also took comfort in the "eight inches of steel armor" around him.

While Fireman Highfill could not and did not know that only one pump was now operating, he did have to concede there was "no safe place on a ship."

At 1351 the infinitely complex gyrocompass system—both gyros—went completely out, indicating that more electric "brain" panels and circuit breakers had failed. It was unlikely that they could be repaired.

At 1400 the *Lexington* hauled a few additional compass points toward the southeast, into the wind. Speed was reduced to 15 knots in order to land the remaining planes from the strike which had crippled the second enemy carrier following the sinking of the *Shoho* on the preceding day.

136

The *Shokaku,* "Soaring Crane," would soar no farther until after many months back in her "nest"—a repair yard in Japan.

The Navy pilots had a hard flight back, not so much because of the enemy but because of the bad weather—mist as well as rain. Fortunately the task force's homing device, "YE," known affectionately as "hayrake" because of the shape of the transmitting antenna, was still functioning.

"We ran into three separate sections of Jap dive-bombers," Noel Gayler reported, "the wheels-down style, returning from their attack on our own group. I turned around and attacked the first section of them, but the other two I had to let go because I didn't have any gas."

En route, Gayler picked up a message from Bill Ault, the air group commander, advising that his radioman had been seriously wounded, possibly was dead. He himself had been hit in the left arm and leg. His plane, too, was "all shot up."

Unable to fix his position, Ault talked to the *Lexington,* asking for radio directions. In a few more minutes he reported he was ditching, then added: "Remember, we got a 1,000-pound hit on the flattop, and one other plane got one, too!"

These were the last words ever picked up from Commander Ault, Annapolis '22. "Red" Gill logged, "He was not [any more] on the [radar] screen."

It echoed of an epitaph.

15

"We are calling for help."

The officer of the deck on the *Russell* noted, "*Lexington* is out of position."

There were yet greater concerns. How could "they" stop the spreading fires?

The mains were cracked. The CO_2, foam and what little other fire-fighting equipment had been available on board was all but exhausted. Still, crewmen struggled ahead in their efforts to save the *Lexington*.

To Noel Gayler, who with only one other plane from the strike made it safely through AA fire from the *Yorktown* to his own damaged deck, the carrier paradoxically "looked fine . . . she was leaving a trail of oil, that was about all. She was on even keel. I knew the Japs had hit her, from all that radio traffic, but when I saw her I was very much relieved because I thought she hadn't been seriously hurt.

"She had taken her torpedo hits very nicely, without impairing her essential functions at all. She could handle her aircraft and make her speed and stay into the wind. Apparently the engineers were in pretty good shape and everything else."

The very fact that some of the familiar planes were home infused a renewed assurance into the hearts of the crew. It did not seem to matter greatly that other 'craft were in the sea, their crews finishing the return flight by whaleboat to various ships in the task force. The aircraft that would never come home were out of sight anyhow.

Aviation maintenance men such as Len Olliff concluded that everything most likely was "okay." Even the broken plane barrier encountered by Griffith had been repaired.

However, the ship's own engineers—if "in pretty good shape"—had reason to believe that the situation was far from "okay." Although "Heine" Junker was neither overly optimistic nor pessimistic, he was concerned about getting more repair parties to the core of the fire, the vortex seemingly of all the explosions in the vicinity of the forward elevator. He also remained concerned about rumors that several men trapped in a forward pump room were resignedly playing cards since their lot seemed hopeless.

Conceivably their voices had been heard by Dudley during the attack, applauding the gunners and urging them to yet deadlier marksmanship.

From the fury of the assault, the mood of the *Lexington* was becoming weary and, to some, dazed. There was apprehension as to whether the ship would remain afloat—but no longer the terror from being shot at and bombed.

Stanley Johnston, existing in a sort of reportorial limbo with no say in either the defense or salvation of the ship, evinced scant illusions as to what would likely happen.

"The fires," he wrote, "could not be shut off any longer, nor could they be extinguished with water, because the explosion had shattered the water mains that fed the fire hoses on these decks. Pumps—small, electrically operated auxiliary pumps that were scattered all over the ship to provide pressure in any area—were useless without water.

"Then, before extra lengths of hose could be led in from undamaged sections of the ship, the fires consumed the electric mains, cutting off light and power where they were needed most. Hoses from remote auxiliary pumps still operating did not supply nearly enough water. . . .

"By this time the engineers were aware that the main fire was being fed from huge storage tanks in a section which could not be flooded."

Each explosion weakened the bulkheads surrounding the gasoline tanks within the ship's innards, allowing more of the fuel to escape. It was directly ignited or vaporized in the mounting heat inside the *Lexington,* then exploded with devastating effect like an air-gasoline mixture within the cylinders of an automobile engine.

Thus, the explosions were self-perpetuating. By warping or knocking holes in the bulkheads, the blasts allowed air to circulate. The onrush of oxygen set smoldering material into crackling flame. In turn, the fires were ready to ignite the next mass of vapor.

The settling of the ship, too, as she took on more water and began to list anew, pushed up successive quantities of gasoline to the top of the broken tanks, which then spilled over, like a pitcher left under a running faucet.

Meanwhile, smoke rolling into the infirmary was making it uninhabitable.

"Communications circuits were dead," Dr. White, bruised but at work, continued his report. "All patients and personnel were ordered to put on gas masks because of smoke and fumes, and all were able to make their way to the captain's cabin (under the flight deck near the starboard AA battery) where a first-aid station had already been established.

"The transfer was accomplished very effectively by the corpsmen and the musicians, under the supervision of Chief Pharmacist's Mate R. A. Fleming. Casuals in the vicinity of the CPO quarters, which were badly damaged by the blast, were brought to the main deck station.

141

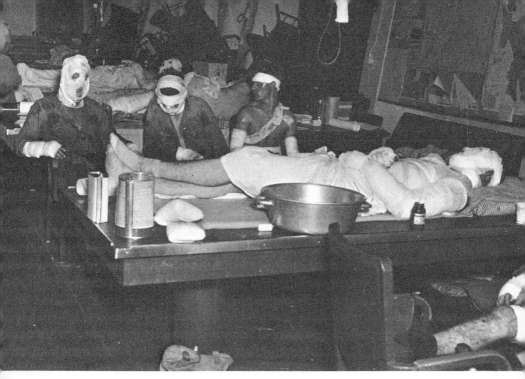

This scene was photographed aboard a small carrier later in World War II, but it was typical on ship after ship following most major clashes at sea. Burn cases were usually treated on mess hall tables or ward room tables (as here).　　　NATIONAL ARCHIVES

"Supplies were also brought up from the operating room by this repair party. Blood plasma, tannic acid jelly and morphine were available, thanks to the good old water beakers and thermos jugs which had been kept filled for many months as standby supply. Lemons and oranges made available from messes supplemented the limited water supply, and due to the watchful care of Chaplain Markle, no one suffered from lack of water or fruit juice.

"In this group, severe burns predominated, the cases numbering about twenty. One case showed severe injury to left leg, probably a fracture of the femur. Two cases showed delirium, one of which had a laceration of scalp with possible basal fracture.

"Work was progressing satisfactorily at this station until the spreading fires belowdeck began to fill the cabin with smoke. Efforts were made to check it by closing doors into

142

the passageways and cutting off dampers in the ventilating trunk.

"All efforts failed and it soon became necessary to move all patients to the 5-inch gun gallery, starboard side, and very soon from there to the flight deck."

Joe Hart, still wondering if his brother Tom were safe, watched the rescue parties going below. Some of them, or members of them, he never saw return. "I'm no coward," he thought. Still, he could not convince his legs to obey his mind and start again into that boiling crater belowdecks.

Edward V. Fox, a fireman first class from Wawatosa, Wisconsin, of the "Milwaukee group," and another member of a brother "team" aboard the *Lexington,* had taken position on the stack, where Joe Hart's brother had been stationed. There he learned of the death of Tom Hart and saw also one of his own friends, mortally wounded, being carried down.

Edward's brother, David, a yeoman, remained at his AA-gun station.

Below, Fox's friend, Erich Eger, found conditions yet worse when he resumed "just trying to find casualties." The fire, he reasoned, kept "but one compartment away." The multiple layers of paint would puff out into blisters—or "red balls," as "Willie" Williamson saw them—and explode. Then Eger and his companions would move to another compartment.

The carrier, he concluded, "must have good watertight integrity" to remain afloat.

The young Milwaukeean was kept company in his prowls by others, some of whom were much more careless of their own safety. Ed Muhlenfeld witnessed a mess steward, whom he recognized, bringing two men up from a "bad" area. The steward, who Muhlenfeld never considered "a very good one," already had suffered possibly second-degree burns.

"Don't go back down," Muhlenfeld advised, although he did not order. "There are hot shells."

"I just got to get my buddies," the steward insisted, and was gone again.

143

Soon he reappeared with more burns on his arms and chest, also with two more men. Muhlenfeld hoped the steward would win a Navy Cross for his heroism.

Junker, methodically glancing at his wristwatch, estimated that more or less minor explosions were occurring "intermittently forward, at periods of about every twenty minutes," with the new development of "white smoke . . . emitted around the side of the band room doors, indicating gasoline explosions."

Johnston, the correspondent, scribbled "The end."

Even so, "Red" Coward, for one, thought "it all looked good" so far. The commander of sky aft, however, was compelled to alter his mental assessment at 1443, just two minutes prior to quarter of three o'clock, by Dudley's log, when there occurred a "heavy explosion under forward elevator."

The navigator's log continued: "Lost steering control on bridge. All radios out of commission. Steering by after steering station, using sound power telephone to order setting for rudder."

The carrier was normally "conned" electrically, with "finger-tip" control, much as an automobile with power steering. The helm on the bridge actuated motors deep inside the stern of the long carrier. These in turn moved hydraulic rams connected to the massive multiton rudder.

Now, with the electrical cables burned through and/or the circuit breakers scarred and twisted beyond repair, the *Lexington* was steered by phoning directions on a very undependable circuit to a man on the auxiliary or "trick" wheel, not much different or fancier than the helm of any ancient square-rigger.

This key man, positioned in front of the rudder post, was necessarily operating blind, wholly dependent on what someone far topsides—in another world insofar as he was concerned—told him to do. His every response this way or the opposite was an act of faith.

If something less than an efficient way to navigate one

144

of the world's largest warships, at this moment it was nonetheless the *only* way.

At 1445 the destroyer *Anderson,* under Lieutenant Commander John K. B. Ginder, Class of '23, from Altoona, Pennsylvania, received from the *Lexington*: "Serious explosion occurred on this ship."

At the same time, the keeper of the signal log on the *Lexington* recorded, "We are calling for help." Then, prudently, all entries in this communications log ceased. There were more urgent, and in some cases personal matters at hand.

At 1450 the *Lexington* signaled the *Anderson,* "Stand by to render assistance."

At eight minutes before 1500 hours, "Red" Gill, the fighter director, logged, "Flames on *Lexington* are not under control. We are unable to service aircraft on the deck. Our radar was temporarily out when the power went off the gyro control."

One minute later, there was, by the navigator's log, "a heavy explosion under forward elevator."

This blast slammed the elevator, already inoperable, down a foot, just as Fred Hartson was pushing a plane across it. The erratic elevator immediately surged upward again, throwing another man off it and onto a gunmount, just as Hartson jumped clear.

"Rip" Raring, concerned all the while that he himself had been unable to do "a damn thing worthwhile," believed it went up two feet. Duckworth estimated but six inches. From his elevation on the "island" he could observe flames spewing out "around the edges."

Conley Cain, taking a look in the same direction, saw "a caldron of flames" below. But to Ed Muhlenfeld it appeared as though the elevator merely had "hiccuped."

Williams, the supply officer, aware that "a good many storekeepers who were on ammunition hoists were killed and no one was able to get back down," remained "a little bit worried" about the third of a million dollars in the fire-surrounded safes. He was on his way to the bridge passing near the elevator at the time. He wanted to be sure the captain understood that he had "done everything I could" to get at the safes.

"I got back," he reported, "and got a running start and ran over between explosions and got up to the bridge to try to tell the captain that I wasn't able to get the money off.

"There was nothing the captain was less interested in, I guess, at the time, so the officer of the deck wouldn't let me up to see him—but I had done my duty, I think. I knew I couldn't get the money off."

"Mort" Seligman ordered a hose "from aft" led to the top of the elevator. Some pressure was teased out of it, and he noted "the water seemed to have some effect on the fire in the well." He added:

"I asked Carpenter Nowack to ensure that all hangar deck sprinklers were turned on, and Lieutenant Commander O'Donnell saw that the "ready" torpedo warheads on the mezzanine were sprinkled.

"The hangar deck was very hot and the fire was slowly spreading aft, although the hose forward appeared to have assisted in the elevator well as steam was evident."

However, "explosions in the vicinity of the elevator well recurred every few minutes."

Thus, it became less and less surprising to Dudley to hear Captain Sherman repeat what he had already uttered, "If we could only get that fire out!"

One deck above him, Admiral Fitch on his flag bridge felt the same way. "One explosion," he thought, "might have blown up the whole damn business—and nearly 3,000 people."

And yet, the former captain of the *Lexington* could not take his staff off, even though he rationalized there was probably every "reg" reason to do so—a task force commander risking himself and his staff.

Only one officer of that staff, in fact, found words to express what probably all of that little flag group were thinking:

"Admiral, don't you think we better get off?"

Fitch drew himself up to his full 5 feet 6 inches, looked at his subordinate, then said nothing.

"The dense fuel oil smoke finally became so bad," it was apparent to "Heine" Junker, "that the repair parties had to abandon these [forward] compartments. All doors and hatches were closed before abandoning. Dead and wounded on the hangar deck were moved [farther] aft. Hangar deck was filling rapidly with a dense, brown smoke.

"Although exhaust blowers on hangar deck were running, they were not of sufficient capacity to exclude all the smoke. This smoke was being discharged through the hangar deck exhaust blowers on the port side to the boat pockets, where it was drawn back into the engineering spaces by the intake blowers which are located in the same boat pockets.

"The spaces were filling with smoke, so intake blowers were shut down. This caused the spaces to become unbearably hot."

Vernon Highfill, who thought "hell broke loose" during the attack, had reason to believe it was still amuck.

"The ship was on fire everywhere," he would recall, "and the lights and power went off down in the engine rooms and it was getting so hot with the blowers off that some of the men were passing out. I was told that it was 157° in the forward engine and pump room.

"We had fires on top of us and side of us, and everything was blowing up and we couldn't put out the fires or cool down the engine room.

"I ate lots of salt tablets and drank a lot of water but that did not help much. So I took off all my clothes except my pants, trying to keep cool. I even stood under water coming out from a water tank."

The very sight of smoke "pouring out from belowdecks" was sufficient to cause those such as Harold Littlefield to rationalize that the carrier was "in serious trouble." With what the fire-fighting crews had to work with, he believed, by now "it was a pretty hopeless job."

It seemed all the more preposterous that gunners' mates were compelled to circulate throughout the carrier warning the crew against smoking cigarettes, cigars and pipes. Gasoline vapors continued to mingle with the smoke from the fires.

But most of the caution, even blunt orders, fell on deaf ears. The men, in their nervousness, kept lighting up anyhow.

"Rip" Raring, himself a heavy smoker, knew the carrier was in serious trouble as he watched a seaman holding a hose over a 1,000-pound bomb which was smoking from the heat. Not a single drop could be coaxed from the nozzle. This he "sensed" as a "disquieting thing."

Gunner's mate Harden personally defused some of the carrier's aerial bombs, although others of smaller size sizzled red then white hot and blew to bits with a deafening Wham!, showering shrapnel around the area for many yards. When hoses were played onto them, they steamed alarmingly.

The "water curtains" of the hangar deck, similar to an overhead sprinkler system, were turned on full. A small, "ineffectual quantity of water," by Duckworth's measure, was "delivered," scarcely enough to show on the hot deck plates.

Dr. Roach, who had been observing the "violent fire" under the elevator, finally saw the deck plates in the surrounding area glow "cherry red." Water supply to the forward hoses had completely failed, as had the pressure on the lines leading to the ammunition hoists and, in fact, the entire sprinkling system.

As Seligman noted, "explosions continued with increasing frequency in various sections. The main deck forward was completely impassable.

"The situation became momentarily more desperate.

"The forward part of the ship was ablaze, both above and below the armored deck, with absolutely no means left to fight the fire which was now spreading aft on the hangar deck. It was inevitable that the twenty-odd torpedo warheads on the mezzanine of the hangar deck must eventually detonate."

O'Donnell was advised that "ready ammunition" of the 5-inch batteries still intact "was getting very hot." The gunnery officer then ordered "all ready 5-inch ammunition thrown over the side." He was informed that some of it was so hot that it could not be handled "with bare hands." Torpedo warheads on the mezzanine of the hangar were just as hot.

Communications with the hangar which, as Duckworth noted, "had been intermittent for some time due to the large quantities of smoke" finally ceased altogether. Now it was abandoned and, again, Dr. Roach had to supervise the transfer of his wounded to yet another make-do sick bay—this time to the flight deck.

"It was necessary," wrote Dr. White, "to abandon the process of hoisting the wounded to the main deck because it was feared that the torpedo warheads might explode. The remaining wounded were then carried, without stretchers, up the ladder to the torpedo gallery, through the ship fitters' shop, thence up to the main deck."

"When we left the hangar deck," said Dr. Roach, "the entire forward end was a mass of flames and the smoke was so dense that it was impossible to see more than a foot or two even with a strong flashlight. We were fortunate in finding our way out simply by feeling our way."

Dr. White again could attest that Dr. Roach and his assistants had accomplished their mission "with utter disregard for their own safety." But many problems remained. For example, as the chief surgeon added, "with lack of clothing, covering of any type, mostly sheets, chair covers and spreads were used."

He also regretted that "injured personnel had to be moved so frequently."

Now only those protected by oxygen masks and fire-retardant clothing could enter any portion of the hangar deck. And surely there was a shocking insufficiency of these essentials.

Captain Sherman himself "remained on the bridge to direct the handling of the ship and to receive reports." Commander Seligman, he observed, "was everywhere, advising and encouraging the firefighters. Small explosions of ammunition were occurring frequently in the vicinity of the fires."

149

The executive officer once more was blown "from water-tight doors through which he was passing." But he picked himself up each time and "brought to the bridge frequent reports of conditions down below."

There, "all lights were out and the damage-control men toiled in complete darkness except for hand flashlights. The decks where they were working would grow hot from fires on the decks beneath.

"Despite the loss of our rudder indicator on the bridge, we were able to steer from there for a while. It was during this period that we landed the torpedo squadron which returned so late and which we had feared was lost. Then the electric steering gear went completely out and we had to steer by maneuvering the engines, giving orders to the engine room over the one telephone still working. We were unable to use the hand steering in the station below * for lack of communications to give the steersman there his course.

"The fire continued to spread. More frequent explosions were occurring, and the surface of the elevator in the flight deck was beginning to glow a dull red.

"A report came from the engine control room that the forward engine-room bulkhead was getting white hot, and that the temperature in that vicinity had risen to 160°. They asked permission, which I promptly granted, to abandon the forward engine room and use only the after engine room space."

"Heine" Junker assumed the full duties of Commander "Pop" Healy, lost apparently in central station but still officially "missing." Noting that four repair parties were still in action—although he feared that a fifth, forward, had been caught in the elevator explosion and wiped out—he rationalized that he at least had the means to retard the fires and explosions.

If he could not help to save the carrier, the engineer officer figured, he might be able to keep her afloat long enough to effect the rescue of all the crewman who were alive.

---

* "trick" wheel.

"At this time," he reported, "telephone communication was still maintained with repair parties 1, 3, 4 and 5.

"All spare men and rescue breathers available were sent forward. I ordered Lieutenant Hawes with Repair 4 to take over the duties of Repair 2 and to fight the fire aft, but not to open up closed compartments, especially the machine shop, hoping that the fire might burn itself out.

"Explosions forward continued at intervals of twenty to thirty minutes."

Hank Laupan, who had been overcome in Nowack's party, realized, when he heard of the missing Repair 2, that he too might have been "a casualty" were it not for his "squeeze box." The desire of one of the petty officers in Repair 4 to take lessons on Laupan's small accordion had been the inspiration for the Wisconsin boy's transfer from No. 2 to No. 4 Party.

With little rest, Erich Eger, following successive new explosions "not only attempted to fight fire" with members of his repair party "but also tried to reach various areas which might possibly contain additional personnel who were by this time without communications."

The machine shop remained critical since 1,000-pound aerial bombs were stored there. In a carrier, only the vessel's own ammunition rated the luxury of storage in actual magazines. The planes' assorted weaponry was slung, hung and stacked wherever there seemed to be a few square feet or, hopefully, yards of space, sort of like a naval curio shop.

The *Lexington*, racked by the forward explosions, was "down by the head." Planes were shoved farther aft on the teakwood flight deck, itself smoking as the flames below tended to make it like a grill. The relatively insignificant weight of the remaining aircraft, less than a dozen, did not compensate for the lowering bow.

At 1500 the *Anderson* noted that she had "closed" the *Lexington*. The destroyer adjusted her speed, approximately 100 yards abeam, and awaited further orders.

Two minutes later, the carrier "broke breakdown flag, speed slackening."

16

"Get the boys off!"

As though *Lady Lex* were stubbornly unwilling to die, even *in extremis,* she lurched toward the southwest at nearly 17 knots. Half the powerful vessel's "top," it was nonetheless no inconsequential speed.

Yawing because of the ever-compounded steering problems, the carrier, even as the *Morris* logged, was surely on an "erratic" course. The most lubberly could recognize that.

"Open out formation about the *Lexington,*" Admiral Fletcher signaled, "and disregard her movements!"

He was worried lest the stricken ship careen into others of the task force.

At 3:20 P.M. the heat in the forward "A" machinery space forced the abandonment of the area. Sweating, weak, half-sick under temperatures approaching 160° F., the crew "secured" the machinery by pulling switches.

Five minutes later an "extra-heavy explosion," by Dudley's measure, "port side amidships," sent "heavy black smoke pouring out of the stack."

Communications to the after "trick" wheel were lost.* Not only were the wires to all phones seemingly burned and the circuit breakers open, but the brass speaking tube as well

---

* The sequence of how the wounded *Lexington* was steered remained somewhat hazy in the memory of her survivors, nor did the log, rescued by the carrier's navigating officer, resolve all questions during the last few hours. It is likely, however, that steering was attempted by speeding up one propeller and slowing others on alternate sides even while the crude "trick wheel" astern was in operation.

was apparently melted. Now a chain of "repeaters" was established, men distributed within hearing of one another along the some 450 feet of usable if smoky passageways and ladders extending astern and below from the bridge.

This meant a considerable delay in relaying commands to turn the rudder, which was turtle-like enough in "obeying." However, it *should* work.

Sherman again asked his navigating officer to plot a course to Australia—most likely for Townsville, some 400 miles west. Then, since the signal lights were inoperative, the captain ordered a flag semaphore query to the *Morris* asking "if fire hose could be passed if *Lexington* steered steady course?"

The *Morris* logged this at 3:30.

At the same time, Durant, the acting supply officer, moved the remainder of his crew from the "untenable" smoke-filled galleys, bringing with them all the fruit and sandwiches they could carry. Cans of water, which had been placed at various stations about the ship, were "moved off" because by now the water was hot and stale.

At 1538, the *Hammann* ordered the *Anderson* to "take station ahead of *Lexington*."

Two minutes later the quartermaster's log of the *Lexington* recorded: "Established telephone communication with after steering by relay through main control over JV telephone. Smoke forced the abandonment of stations on stack, also air plot and communication stations."

Four minutes later, "Another explosion on port side."

And at 1545, "Abandon sky forward and surface forward."

At 1548, "Lost all pressure on fire main aft."

Junker, who had been ordering one fire room, boiler room and machinery space after another abandoned, would write:

"The watch in the forward machinery space are to be commended for their devotion to duty, having remained at their stations operating A and B units for a period of about one hour after all electric light and power had been lost. No blowers were operating during this period and the smoke and heat became unbearable.

154

"A great percentage of this watch was so exhausted that they required assistance of others in leaving this space."

At the same time, a corpsman was struggling up from his dressing station in the reserve plane stowage compartment, which had become filled with smoke:

". . . We put on our gas masks, lost indirect communication with the bridge. There were no casualties in our area and all personnel departed, going to flight deck through the fuselage deck where there was much smoke, much dripping hot water from the sprinkler system and poor visibility with only three electric lights on.

"There were three ways of leaving and everyone should have gotten to the flight deck."

All the first-aid stations and the patients were being transferred up from the oven-like interior of the carrier to the flight deck. Chaplain Markle helped evacuate the captain's cabin, which had been used as an emergency dressing station, now suffocating with "billowing black smoke."

". . . We moved our men out on the gun galleries but had to move from there so the guns could be effectively fired if another attack was made. We passed the wounded on up a makeshift ladder to the flight deck. Some were in horrible shape.

"We had to leave there so the planes could use the deck, however. Finally we moved them behind the stack.

"I asked Dr. White if he thought all patients were out and he was uncertain because there were so many. Dr. White and I each put on a gas mask and went [back] to the captain's cabin and felt our way around, but neither of us could locate anyone.

"We then were almost certain that all were clear."

Two minutes before four o'clock there were several "minor explosions" under the forward elevator. The quartermaster logged: "Fire on main deck out of control. Communications to main control growing very faint."

Sherman himself reported: "All lights forward were out and the main deck and below were full of smoke. It was a losing fight to control the fire.

155

"The one remaining phone working the main control was getting very weak. It was apparent that it was only a matter of time until it would go out completely. When it did, I realized, there would be no way of getting the men out of the engine rooms. Unless I ordered them to leave, they would stay there, trapped by fire all around them, and hemmed in by red-hot bulkheads, until they perished.

" 'A' unit's bulkhead was so hot the paint was peeling off in large blisters.

"Over the weakening phones I ordered these men to secure the engineering plant and get up on deck. Although we were unable to hear any reply, presently the sound of steam escaping from the safety valves assured me they had received the message.

"We now had no power and the ship lay dead in the water."

Sherman advised Fletcher, "Have lost pressure, fire out of control. List increasing. Have abandoned all below stations."

The captain had also abandoned all hope of somehow steaming through the Great Barrier Reef—with only a skeleton crew aboard—and beaching the carrier. Then there might have been a chance of extinguishing the flames.

It was time for the senior officer to reassume tactical command of what was left of the air group and of the aerial operations. And that is what Admiral Fletcher did.

Admiral Fitch had thought it "a very generous thing" earlier when Fletcher, senior to him if slightly younger, had given him command for the approaching action.

According to Junker, "the fire room, engine room and repair 4 and 5 parties escaped thrrough the boiler intakes direct to the main deck. Main control, ice machine, motor room and number 1 and 2 torpedo air compressor personnel escaped through the ladders on the starboard side leading up past the refrigerator spaces."

Others from below attained safety via scuttles, vents and other emergency passages.

When Vernon Highfill "left the engine room and started

156

up the ladder to the next deck," the cooler air "hit me and I passed out just for a second. When I snapped out of it I took off, running toward the smokestack.

"I went up through the smokestack to the flight deck. The stack has a little space between the smoke and the outside that you can go through without getting burned.

"When I reached the flight deck and looked over I saw a hole in the deck big enough to put a house in and a few guns lying around. I didn't have any time to look on the left side to see any of the holes. There was an officer and he was telling everybody to go over the side."

It was 4 P.M. in the Coral Sea—eight bells—and the *Lexington* was going.

She was "stopped," logged the *Morris;* the *Anderson* "commenced circling"; the *Morris* cautiously drew along the starboard side of the stricken carrier.

Like practically all of his shipmates, Radioman Littlefield was aware that the carrier had "come to a halt. . . . It was apparent that we were going to have to leave the 'Old Lady.' "

Another operator abruptly put down the "fox tail" brush with which he had been idly dusting his transmitter.

"Rip" Raring, treasurer of the officers' "cigar mess," which dispensed tobacco, candy and soft drinks, decided it was past time to fetch the approximately $500 cash in his cabin as well as his class ring. He was able to feel and cough his way through the smoke to obtain the money and the ring, although the cabin was by this time "ankle deep in water." When returning to deck, Raring was consumed by a feeling of unreality as he watched the great ship "rolling this way and that."

As Captain Sherman and the overwhelming majority of his shipmates had already reacted, he thought the best thing to do was light up another cigarette. What was a little more smoke, now?

"Ted" Sherman, the scrappy boxer of midshipman days, conceded that he had lost this round.

"In case it is necessary to abandon ship," he advised Admiral Fletcher, "have ship stand by to recover personnel."

157

"Pat" Dowling "received orders from the executive officer to lower life rafts from the stowage position on the stack and distribute them forward and aft, where they could be launched if necessary." These were 8 feet wide and doughnut-shaped, of balsa wood with latticed decking.

The onetime bos'n was frustrated, however, by his inability to lower the two power boats—one fifty feet, the other forty—housed in "pockets" or alcoves on the port and starboard sides, aft, below the gun galleries. Unlike the whaleboats that could be hand-lowered, the big motor launches were wholly dependent on the electric motors that worked the heavy davits.

"Men were detailed from the third division to prepare the rafts on the port side of the ship for lowering, and men from the first and fourth divisions were detailed to lower boats."

The *Morris* was alongside to starboard at 1615.

Meanwhile, on the *New Orleans,* Chaplin Forgy had spent an afternoon of "intermittent anxiety" as the fleet "raced southward." He had been listening to "one long succession of reports.

"First, the fires on the *Lexington* were under control. Then fires on the *Lex* had broken out anew. Then they were under control again, and so it went. Gradually the smoke clouds coming from the giant carrier became more and more dense, and the pace of our task force became slower and slower.

"The *Lexington* was dead in the water now. I saw hundreds of her men milling about her deck. They leaned obliquely to starboard to fight the steep port list of the ship. We moved in closer until she was less than a thousand yards away.

"I saw angry tongues of orange flame against the black smoke. From under her bridge a jet cloud funneled hundreds of feet into the air.

"On her deck were helmeted officers and enlisted men and the helpless-looking torpedo planes, bombers and fighters crowded together aft.

"I went up to the bridge and looked at the fascinating yet tragic scene through the telescope. I saw corpsmen bringing stretchers to the deck. Men were tying lifebelts about themselves. Cargo nets were being dropped over the side."

Captain "Gib" Hoover, the destroyer squadron comman-der aboard the *Morris,* waved to Admiral Fitch looking down at him from the carrier's flag bridge. When the two task forces rendezvoused, Fitch had radioed to Hoover, "Hope we have the same luck we had in the last war."

The two had served in 1918 on the battleship *Wyoming,* on which Fitch was a gunnery officer with the Grand Fleet.

Jarrett, commanding the *Morris,* which was rather top-heavy, thought the destroyer was a poor choice to be so close to the carrier. The gun tubs or blisters jutting from the sides of the *Lexington* kept smashing into the bridge and superstructure of the little *Morris.*

Nonetheless, both electric lines and hoses were thrown over to the carrier and boards were placed between the sterns of the two ships for bringing off the wounded, who were al-ready being assembled. In fact, Dr. White was busy at an impromptu operating table removing shrapnel and tying off "bleeding vessels" when it was time to start the transfer of patients.

Dr. White, in worsening shape from his shoulder and ankle injuries, ordered one last search "throughout the adjacent area of the battle-dressing station and the compartments used for hospitalization, and no living personnel were found."

At the same time the chief surgeon reminded himself that he must formally commend the musicians, traditional Navy helpmates in battle, for their "efficient, resourceful and tire-less" work as stretcher-bearers and for performing other emergency services for the injured and dying.

As the first patients were carried in stretchers along the heaving gangplank, "Beany" Jarrett thought, "Gee, some of those birds are burned head to foot!"

Then he ducked as a small explosion on the carrier blew flaming debris across the top decking of the *Morris.*

Lieutenant (jg) Ray Laird, who had abandoned his for-ward gunnery position, was hard at work by the starboard whaleboat davits, which had become "the primary abandon ship station for all wounded." He was getting the casualties off "by means of my whaleboats at first, finally by lowering

159

The crew wanders the deck of the *Lexington,* waiting to abandon.

The *Morris* stands alongside of the *Lexington* to aid evacuation of the wounded giant's crew.   NATIONAL ARCHIVES

Survivors of the *Lexington* climb aboard one of the carrier's escort vessels. NATIONAL ARCHIVES

loaded Stokes stretchers with the davits into other boats, and in last instances by sliding loaded stretchers down pieces of staging to the bridges of the daring destroyers whose captains had guts enough to come alongside despite the fact that the *Lex* was disintegrating."

The first boat hailed the *Hammann* at 1619.

"Additional explosions were occurring," noted Captain Sherman. "It was reported that the warheads on the hangar deck had been at a temperature of 140° F., ready bombs storage was in the vicinity of the fire and I considered there was danger of the ship blowing up any minute.

"Without pressure on the main, we were helpless even to fight the fire. I ordered life rafts made ready and preparations to abandon ship . . . the fire pumps from the *Morris* were of such low capacity that only a trickle of water could be obtained from this source.

"It seemed outrageous that we could do nothing to put out the fire and save our ship!"

Dudley figured it was worse than outrageous. The pressure from the hoses actually spread the flames.

All squadron personnel were ordered aft to assemble on the deck by their planes. One of them, Hoyt Mann, who had flown off before the decks became unusable, looked down from his circling SBD bomber and experienced a forlorn feeling of helplessness: ". . . All we could do was watch her burn and explode and the [initial] efforts to abandon ship."

The *Hammann*, having picked up the first lifeboat, now bore in closer to the *Lexington*, asking, "Shall I circle clockwise or counterclockwise?"

"Clockwise!"

The task force commander, Fletcher, still not satisfied that *Hammann* was pushing in fast enough, flashed, "Are you coming around to pick up wounded? Speed it up!"

"The fire slowly spread aft," noted Duckworth, "and finally reached the torpedoes on the hanger deck mezzanine."

He could agree with Sherman that the carrier was in mounting danger of "blowing up any minute." When one gunner's mate asked another, "Wonder what temperature them warheads'll have to get before they blow?" his shipmate replied gruffly, "I don't care what the temperature is, I just want to know *when*."

Now, with an increased sense of urgency, Sherman at 1634 requested: "*Anderson* and *Hammann* come alongside. Prepare to pass fire hoses from your pumps!"

Three minutes-later, the *Hammann* advised the *Anderson*: "I will pass astern of you."

"The critically and seriously injured," Dr. White would report, "were lowered over the starboard side in Stokes stretchers and on an improvised plank platform into motor whaleboats and launches from other ships. Other less injured patients were lowered by a line tied around their trunk to a destroyer alongside."

Unwillingly, protesting, Dr. White himself joined the procession to the *Morris*. It had, however, required a direct order from Captain Sherman, increasingly concerned over the well-being of his surgeon.

Williams, who now clutched a folder of pay records even if he couldn't get to the "pay" itself from the blazing disbursing office, had leaned over the deck and called, "Here, catch these pay records!"

The reply came up: "Yes, toss 'em down!"

"All right."

"And then come on down yourself. We want the disbursing officer, the paymaster, with us!"

And so Williams "slid down a line to the destroyer."

The staunch *Hammann,* which tried to fight the fires of the *Lexington* and rescued many of the carrier's crew, was herself sunk a month later, at Midway, while performing the same heroic services for the crippled *Yorktown*. Her commanding officer, Arnold True, received the Navy Cross.   U.S. NAVY PHOTOGRAPH

At the same time "Beany" Jarrett watched one man with a broken leg, not waiting for assistance, crawling down the plank on all fours. The commanding officer himself rushed over and helped him the remaining distance. The destroyer's surgeon, Lieutenant (jg) Norbert J. Schulz, had already set up his emergency hospital in the wardroom.

At 1645 Dudley recapitulated: "Water played on fire around forward elevator without success in extinguishing fire. With loss of speed, a port list of 3° developed and ship took trim down by the bow of about two feet."

Seven minutes later, "Ordered all squadron and air department personnel and men not needed for working the ship to embark on USS *Morris* alongside.

"Large cloud of steam and smoke came up from forward elevator."

At 1700, "List to port now 5°."

The arrival of the vanguard of the flying personnel augmented the growing passenger list aboard the *Morris* to several hundred. One officer, upon his arrival, asked of Jarrett: "Sir, may I keep all of my men together?"

Then another explosion "which blew an 8-inch hole in the side of the carrier opposite the CPO quarters," sent the survivors scurrying and crawling toward the opposite side of the destroyer. The slim vessel nearly capsized.

"All sit down!" Jarrett ordered through his bullhorn. They were obedient and meek enough for the most part, he thought, "in a kind of daze."

In spite of the best in discipline and willingness to obey,

conditions aboard the *Morris* were chaotic, somewhat anal-
ogous to the confusion attending the final cargo onto a tramp
freighter. From his flag bridge, "Gib" Hoover watched with
mixed emotions as AA ammunition was trundled down the
shaky plank. It was needed by all vessels of the task force
after the heavy barrage thrown at them by the morning's
attackers.

Then another heavy explosion occurred opposite the *Morris'* bridge.

The *Anderson* and the *Hammann,* meanwhile, continued
closing, as they received from Fletcher, "condition of *Lexington* follows: Lost all power. Fire not under control. No
change for the better."

Then, the *Anderson* was advised, "If you are on port side,
take that side."

A minute later, the *Anderson* "proceeded to go alongside
port side of *Lexington*." Her starboard bow hit the carrier
—"no damage. Backed away, preparatory to making another attempt. Was unable to stay alongside. *Lexington* had
about a 3° list to port."

The *Hammann* then queried, "*Anderson, w*ere you able to
make port side?"

"Affirmative."

At 1707 Rear Admiral Fitch leaned over his flag bridge
and said calmly: "Well, Ted, let's get the boys off the ship."

Sherman, looking up, thought Fitch extremely "unper-
turbed and efficient." Nonetheless, the order was "heart-
breaking." To Stanley Johnston, nearby, there was "nothing
dramatic" in the admiral's terse command.

The captain did concede "it seemed the only thing left to
do." Then, "reluctantly," he gave the order.

The nearby destroyers read the flag hoist their individual
signalmen had been anticipating for the past hour or more:

"I am abandoning ship!"

17

"I got to thinking about the propellers . . ."

Through "the long glass," Chaplain Forgy on the *New Orleans,* "saw a couple of men dive clear from the deck to the sea. Others were climbing down the cargo nets now, and I could see heads bobbing about in the water.

"The *No-Boat* cautiously edged closer to the *Lexington.* The speaker broke the air with words we had hoped never to hear: 'The *Lexington* has been compelled to abandon ship. Stand by to rescue survivors!'"

"Frenchy" Landis was "pleasantly surprised" at the captain's order. He had thought all along that only the wounded would make it off onto the destroyers.

At the same time the gregarious aviation "mech" experienced fleeting disappointment that the carrier would not be limping into Australia for "drawn-out" repairs. He'd heard about the good times there on shore leave.

At 1710 the quartermaster of the *Lexington* affirmed, "All hands abandon ship!"

And to be absolutely certain, Captain Sherman stood on a bridge wing and shouted through his megaphone, "All right now, all hands put the rafts over the side and abandon ship!"

"Frenchy" did not have to be told twice. He braced himself under the weight of a chief with a broken leg, whose arm was around his shoulder, and walked down the plank to the *Morris*. He thought all the while how ridiculously simple it was.

"Frenchy" turned once and decided he "felt bad" to have to leave "all those planes behind."

He did not have much more time. Seaman were hauling in the hoses and electric lines preparatory to casting off. A few more from the carrier made it, with only seconds to spare, including Vernon Highfill, who slid down a rope onto the *Morris'* deck.

Now, still naked save for his begrimed and sweat-drenched underpants, the fireman could sit down and wonder just *how,* after his escape through the stack, he happened to be alive.

The *Morris* logged at 1714, "All available deck space now occupied by survivors, and 300 in water. Life rafts and whaleboat from *Minneapolis*. Searchlight and windscreen on bridge smashed."

It was "a horrible sight as we backed away," recalled Lieutenant Williams, "because there were some in the water behind the destroyer. They had over 700 men on the destroyer and they had to get away from the carrier because they were afraid that the explosions would break through the flight deck and cause the destroyer to capsize.

"They had the horrible choice of perhaps cutting up a man or two in the water or staying on there endangering the whole ship. They were very skillful. I don't believe they killed anybody."

Quite the opposite. "Beany" Jarrett was so solicitous that he sent one warrant, a powerful swimmer, over the side to grab one *Lexington* survivor who seemed to be floundering dangerously close by the *Morris*.

170

At 1718 the *Anderson* "lowered port boat into the water. *Anderson* now about 800 yards from the *Lexington*. *Morris* and *Hammann* both were near stern of the *Lexington*."

They were leaving the radio shack. "Most of us," wrote Harold Littlefield, "went down to the flight deck and started breaking out life rafts and carrying them to the bow and to the stern. This was done and the lines run over the side.

"She must have been burning furiously in the hangar deck. As I walked over the elevators several times, dragging life rafts, the deck was very hot and smoke was pouring out.

"Those who were back aft had a treat that we on the bow missed out on. The ice cream locker was aft on the main deck so they broke her open and all the fellows there had all the ice cream they could eat. Although we up forward missed out on the ice cream, we did find a pan of sandwiches and a keg of drinking water in one of the forward gun galleys and proceeded to use them up.

"It seemed a shame that we had to lose her, but we knew that it was too late to think of saving her then, for there was the possibility that she might blow up any time. Before we got off there were several more nasty explosions, but I don't believe anyone was hurt in them. The morale of the men was excellent; I don't remember seeing any sign of panic. In fact, shortly before leaving ship I saw one fellow lying on the flight deck reading a magazine!

"I left the ship over the bow going hand over hand down a line into the water. There was no rushing by anyone and each man waited until the one before him was pretty well down before he started. Several of us got hold of a life raft with one hand and swam with the other, and made out for a destroyer which was lying off our port side.

"The water was nice and warm and apparently there were no sharks around. When we got to the 'cans' they had lines over the side and lifted us aboard.

"As soon as I hit the deck an officer noticed blood on my arm and insisted that I be taken below right away for treatment."

John Wood, unwounded, was concerned only that the listing carrier might "roll over." He moved along the "low" or port side, trying "to avoid the jam," then "grabbed a line and swung over," 60 feet down from the flight deck to the water.

He climbed onto a raft and joined its prior occupants standing waist deep in water. There was "quite a jam of rafts," it was apparent to the radioman from Trout Lake, Washington.

Bemused himself at the spectacle of the crewmen who had "filled their helmets with ice cream," Captain Sherman believed that "the officers and men were as reluctant to leave as I was. . . . Some of them lined up their shoes in orderly fashion on the deck before they left as if they expected to return.

"There was not the slightest panic or disorder. I was proud of them."

Admiral Fitch, descending from the flag bridge, paused to remark to the carrier's commander, "Ted, when the time comes for you to get off I don't want any fancy stuff."

Duckworth interpreted this to mean, "For heaven's sake, don't try going down with your ship or staying until it is too late."

Then Fitch and Sherman, followed by their staffs, left the bridge for the hangar deck. The flag admiral was shocked to see "the dead bodies laid out in rows." Waiting for him was his Marine orderly, holding the admiral's binoculars and a favorite khaki jacket.

"Sir, you go first," the Marine said, saluting.

Fitch told the Marine to put down the jacket as well as the binoculars and "get the hell off the ship!" He added that it was "an order!"

His orderly again saluted Admiral Fitch and did as instructed. Binoculars, like guns, were considered too heavy to take into the water.

The task force commander was surprised at how easy it was to "walk" down the slanting side of the ship, easing himself along the knotted rope. A whaleboat from the *Minneapolis* awaited him below.

172

Sherman, while not contemplating any "fancy stuff," noticed "one crowd . . . at the port after gun gallery. As I approached to see what was delaying them, the men, led by Marine Sergeant Peyton, gave 'three cheers for the captain!'

"Their loyalty was inspiring."

It was understood that this Marine guard would be the last division to quit the carrier in a unit.

Shortly after 1718 the *Anderson* "started receiving aboard personnel of the *Lexington*. Picked them up from the water, from life rafts and from boats."

"At this time," a pharmacist's mate would report, "the carrier was ablaze midships and pouring out tremendous quantities of dense black smoke. There were many explosions of different degrees occurring throughout the ship all during the afternoon and while we were in the water.

"It is felt that no living person remained aboard the ship. All who were there were dead at the time. Those of us who got in the water fared very well, and as far as we could ever determine no life was lost in the water."

To Hartwig, on the *Russell*, it was almost unbearable frustration to stand by as the other destroyers came to the assistance of the *Lexington* and her crew.

"From my screening station with the *Yorktown*," he wrote, "which varied in distance from the *Lex* about 2–8 miles, we hardly took our eyes off her. We saw personnel streaming down lines over the side. We noted a list of about 10 to 15° to port.

"It was extremely difficult indeed to watch from afar, and although I wanted very much to please my crew and request permission to participate in the rescue, it most certainly would have been denied."

Chaplain Forgy observed the wounded being brought up from the first whaleboat to pull alongside the *New Orleans*: ". . . The coxswain, cautiously inching his craft toward the hull of his big ship, turned his head upward and shouted:

" 'They're all badly wounded, sir.'

"Nearly twenty wire baskets were crowded into the boat.

In each basket, helpless under tightly buckled straps, was a wounded man from the *Lexington*.

"A seaman fought against the hull of the *No-Boat* with a boat hook to break the impact as the waves lifted the launch and its pitiful cargo eight or ten feet into the air, then smashed it downward and against the side of the cruiser.

"Sailors in the launch pawed the air to catch the lines tossed overside from the cruiser. The helpless look in the eyes of a wounded lad on one of the stretchers stabbed through me as the lines were made fast at his head and feet and he began the treacherous transfer to the cruiser.

"Dr. Harry Walker reached up to the basket as the seaman eased it to the deck. He spent no more than three seconds looking at the flame-seared man from the carrier. On his forehead a large pink "M" had been painted in Mercurochrome. It told us he had received one injection of merciful morphine before leaving his dying warship.

" 'Take him to sick bay immediately,' Dr. Walker ordered a pair of corpsmen at his side.

"Another casualty was on his way up from the undulating launch. You could see he was unconscious. Soggy splotches of red oozed through the white gauze that bandaged his head. Another wide bandage covered a portion of his naked abdomen.

"Walker looked calculatingly down at the launch and then toward the other boats pushing toward the cruiser.

" 'Bring all these men down to sick bay as fast as they come aboard,' he ordered. Harry knew what to expect, and he ran to join Dr. Evans in sick bay to begin the dreadful task that was to keep him on his feet for the next thirty-six hours.

"The rolling clouds of jet smoke coming from the *Lexington,* now just 500 yards off our port, hid most of her bridge. Her flight deck, leaning in a 20° list, was crowded with more and more men. Some of her crew stood at the edge of the deck, pinched their noses with thumb and forefinger and leaped feet-first to the sea. They looked like kids at home jumping from a diving board."

174

One of those "kids at home," Lester Jones, of Jacksonville, Florida, who had maintained complete confidence in his survival during the attack and also through the afternoon's explosions, tossed mattresses over the starboard bow. Then he casually slid some fifty feet down a line onto one to await the first rescue ship. It was rather pleasant, like floating on an air cushion at the beach, riding up and down on the swells. And so the phlegmatic seaman drifted toward the cradling lines and nets of a waiting destroyer.

Chaplain Markle, with a certain detachment, watched "some [who] simply dived or jumped. As the men left they took off their shoes, and the shoes made an orderly little row along the side of the deck.

"The soda fountain was one flight down and the attendants passed out the ice cream to anyone who wanted it. Several big trays of sandwiches were brought up but they were dry when I saw them and besides I'd lost my appetite."

Shoes and uneaten sandwiches were not all that was left behind on the *Lexington*. Len Olliff, getting ready to slip over the side, noticed the dozens of .45-caliber automatics tossed carelessly onto the smoking flight deck as their owners departed. All flight crews were armed. One man, a Texan, had abandoned even his personal pair of revolvers, with hand-carved grips. He, like the others, did not want to chance their weight, swimming.

Olliff not only "felt badly" about this waste of good sidearms but about his own plane and the now perfect fuel pump he had repaired at such labor all night long. Also, he had never been able to return to his fo'c'sle for his wallet and the various keepsakes, and he had not enjoyed that long-postponed shower bath.

Now, instead, Olliff was going for a swim in the warm Coral Sea.

It was no easy job either getting off the deck or stroking away from the torch-like Gargantua drifting uncontrollably down on those in the water, swimmers and nonswimmers.

Conley Cain worried not only about swimming from the

175

carrier but about sharks "taking a chunk out of my rear," even though he had not observed any. The powerfully built coxswain who had thought to put his billfold, containing $300, in his dungarees pocket, thought he had abandoned quite nicely down a stern line. His only "touchy" moment came when the man above him on the rope kept stepping on his fingers.

Sharks or not, Cain was relieved to be distancing himself from "those 1,000-pound bombs next to the red-hot bulkheads."

His was not a unique annoyance. Everyone seemed to be stepping on other fingers, heads, shoulders or necks—not generally because of any headlong flight from the ship but because of an unfamiliarity with ropes (even if knotted), rope ladders, cargo nets and knotted sheets.

This was not the sailing Navy. Why should sailors be conversant in the mid-twentieth century with hemp and canvas? However, someone on the bridge saw and appreciated the crowding problem, then called through a bullhorn:

"We are *not* sinking, repeat *not*—take your time! Repeat . . . !"

The advice was pertinent in the opinion of Ed Muhlenfeld, going into the water after having been busy dragging rafts from the stack area and also "draping ropes over the side." A seaman above him had actually hung onto the ensign's head with his feet until Muhlenfeld shouted: "Let go!"

The thought coursed through the young officer's mind, "This isn't quite the way we do it in abandon-ship drills. . . ."

"Red" Coward dove into the water. An able swimmer, the erstwhile young commander of sky aft stroked hard parallel to and in the general direction of the bow. As the *Lexington* continued to "overtake" him, he reversed course to 180° aft and swam toward the *Hammann*.

The line they threw him from the destroyer was "too small." It kept sliding through his hands as he clutched it and tried to "walk up" the slimy sides of the *Hammann*. He still wore his rubber-soled shoes, which made his ascent more slippery.

Finally, Coward looped the small-diameter rope about his body and was hauled up onto the deck.

The *Hammann,* as a matter of fact, was just pulling away after several hazardous minutes alongside the carrier.

"It was noted," wrote the destroyer's commander, Arnold True, "that a number of life rafts on the lee side of *Lexington* were caught because wind was drifting the carrier down faster than the rafts could row.

"I took *Hammann* alongside *Lex.* As she drifted down on me, there was great danger that the rafts and men swimming in the water would be crushed between the ships.

"My crew did a wonderful job in getting men and rafts out of the danger area and aboard. Time was so short that they had to act without orders."

After taking aboard the *Lexington* crewmen, including wounded, the destroyer "backed away, which was a difficult maneuver due to the fact that *Lex* was drifting down on *Hammann* as she had been doing on the life rafts.

"The maneuver was successful and we got clear. We were not more than fifty yards away when a magazine on the *Lexington* exploded, blowing out the side of the ship where the *Hammann* had been moored about three minutes before.

"Had we been a few minutes later getting away, the tons of metal thrown out by the explosion would have badly damaged *Hammann* and killed a lot of men."

The explosion, a few minutes before 5:30, which also blew off the quarter deck gangway door, instantly killed Pharmacist's Mate V. L. Weeks, standing nearby on a life raft. Dr. White believed a metal fragment from the door "penetrated his skull."

Lieutenant (jg) Chandler Swanson, from Montclair, New Jersey, who had joined the Navy's aviation cadet program in 1937, was among the pilots caught aboard the helpless ship. Swanson had flown air cover protection until 1 P.M. He was swimming off the carrier's port stern at the time of the tremendous explosion, "which hurled planes and planking over the side and set the deck afire" and also sent a vol-

177

cano-like cloud of smoke mushrooming skyward. Debris was projected over a fifth-of-a-mile radius.

"There were still two balsa rafts," Swanson would report, "with about fifteen men floating at the port quarter. They were being held close to the ship by the suction force, and had been there for about an hour. The situation looked unfavorable for them; fires covered the decks and boat pockets and the explosions increased in number. The big ships were taking their distance and no more small boats were to be seen.

"About ten minutes after the big explosion, the *Lexington's* number 1 motor whaleboat was seen coming around the stern of the sinking carrier. Boatswain's Mate Elbert Hale was making a last checkup of the area near the ship and caught sight of the men by the port quarter. Because of the many lines hanging down from the ship, he signaled the men to come out, but they signaled him to come in because their headway against the suction was practically nil, and he came in, and every man was tumbled into the small boat.

"Hale immediately turned to get clear of the *Lex* but, as he feared might happen, his propeller fouled in one of the lines. The boat, powerless, fell back against the ship and Hale sent one of his crew, Seaman 1st Class B. S. Jeffers, over the side with a sheath knife to clear the propeller. Exhausted, Jeffers was pulled in and Seaman 1st Class H. C. Rowe went over the side to complete the task. The motor was started and the boat headed out from the ship.

"Small-caliber ammunition was going off all along the side of the ship, endangering the lives of those in the boat; on the *Minneapolis,* seven bullet holes were found in it.

"Boatswain's Mate Hale had, unhesitatingly, steered his boat into what was a difficult and dangerous situation to rescue the men in the water at the port quarter."

Another aviator, Lieutenant Gayler, who had heard Bill Ault's last radio message, with "all the aircraft people," had gone into the water "over the quarter [after end]."

178

The explosion, which to Gayler seemed to have come at least from the bomb magazine, "pretty well ripped the ship apart and shook the heavy cruisers at a considerable distance."

Fred Hartson was still concerned vaguely about the "messy" hangar as well as flight deck he was leaving behind. He figured there were about four planes below. He did not know how many were on the flight deck, so many were tilting at crazy angles. But it was time to go in this progression of nearly 3,000 men abandoning ship, which curiously reminded him of "just another drill."

He watched one man inflate an airplane emergency raft, toss it overboard, then execute a graceful dive into the swells beside it. He crawled aboard and paddled off, using his hands.

"I got to thinking about the propeller," Hartson would recall, not sure whether the *Lexington*'s screws were turning over a little or not. He was certain that some men in the water had been crushed by the destroyers' propellers. Rafts were constantly being drawn into the side of the careening carrier or the destroyers.

Since his plane had gone off, anyhow, with his raft, Hartson determined to take his chances in the water.

"I've got to get on the other side," he thought, staring at all the struggling survivors in the lee of the stricken giant. He gained the far, or high side and climbed down onto a "green and slimy torpedo blister," where three others were also clinging—more or less to nothing on the slick, oily sides.

At that instant an apparent explosion knocked some heavy, smoldering chunks of hot cork insulation onto his forehead, which "hurt." He was able to clutch a rivet head as the other three were thrown into the water.

Hartson did not see them reappear.

With his head aching so that he was "almost blind," the aviation machinist worked along the same "slimy" blister

179

toward the bow. He moved himself in that direction since he had heard "an ensign tell the captain that all the torpedo warheads were red hot."

He reasoned that the bow was the safest place if the carrier blew apart midships. Besides, he'd seen most of the remaining flying personnel—air, maintenance and administrative—at the extremities of the deck, fore and aft.

He thought he'd better wait there awhile.

18

"... Cocktail time."

At 1737 "Red" Gill, the fighter director, logged "Another big explosion on *Lex*."

Three minutes later, Admiral Fletcher requested the destroyer command, "Assign two more ships to present operation. Have just one remain with me."

Fred Hartson prepared to quit his precarious perch under the flaring bow. First, he remembered his plastic wallet, still in his trouser pocket. He looked inside, saw it contained three $5 bills. He removed them and tucked them into another pocket, then skimmed the wallet toward the sea.

Next, he jumped off and started dog-paddling.

Joe Hart, who had been helping with the wounded, kept *his* wallet, and several packs of chewing gum, as he quit the *Lexington*. It did not at that moment occur to him that the salt water might have other than a beneficial effect on the gum.

Erich Eger, from Milwaukee, lowered himself down a line. Before he reached the sea, he "saw what a mass of people were in the water," then climbed up on the blister and walked forward to an area where there was a little less confusion. He jumped and struck out for the *Hammann*.

Since the water was warm with "a nice swell" and Eger a good swimmer, the experience was pleasurable enough, even as it had been for Lester Jones.

His friend, Ed Fox, from Wawatosa, worked along the fantail, then grabbed onto one of the many dangling lines and slowly started down it. His brother, Dave, was right behind him, shinnying seaward, hand over hand.

Both reached a raft. In doing so, the younger Dave drank too much of the salt water. This quickly made him sick. As Ed hung onto his "kid" brother, he kept thinking: "God, if I let him go, I'll sure catch hell when I get home. . . ."

Hank Laupan, whose accordion had possibly saved his life, was not far from the rest of the Milwaukee group—which, manifestly, was blessed with magic good fortune.

The signal bridge publications in the pilot house and tactical documents were lashed together and thrown overboard. Confidential communications were packed in "a large, stout bag" and thrown overboard.

Most of the optical equipment and a new blinker tube had been lowered to the *Morris*. Captain Hoover himself had caught a personal telescope tossed down by a quartermaster.

Stanley Johnston, trying to be helpful, picked up a "small leather-cased chronometer" and handed it to Dudley, the navigator. The latter smilingly refused it, explaining, "It hasn't worked for years."

Dudley logged, at 1745, "All injured men on flight deck were lowered over the side to boats and life rafts.

"Only those records which were abovedecks could be saved. Fires in office spaces belowdecks prevented saving of records other than rough deck logs, quartermaster's notebook and rough notes for war diary."

Sherman then took Dudley and his air officer on one of the captain's final tours of inspection. To their surprise, they encountered "some twelve or fifteen wounded men," by Duckworth's count, "alongside the bridge and stack structure." A line was needed to lower them to a whaleboat bobbing below.

"Who's got a knife?" asked the air officer, who had discovered an obvious supply of rope—the "falls" of one of the *Lexington*'s motorboats.

Two other officers who had joined the staff officers and the captain felt their pockets. The results were embarrassing. Finally, Sherman produced one with the wry comment, "I guess I'm the only damned officer with a knife!"

It thereupon turned out that Duckworth was the only "damned officer" who could tie a double bowline knot to afford a "seat" for the wounded.

With the remaining injured lowered off the carrier to boats and rafts, Dudley, accompanied by Duckworth, slid down a rope. The navigating officer knew the time because his watch was "stopped by immersion in salt water at exactly 1745."

Neither the navigating officer nor the air officer was immersed for long. Other survivors pulled the two onto the *Hammann*. The destroyer was close to the stern of the burning *Lexington*, trying to pluck men from rafts caught in the drift of the huge, blazing hulk.

Dudley and Duckworth were still on deck squeezing water out of their uniforms when, as the air officer would report, "Two violent explosions on the flight deck covered the destroyer with debris. On my advice of the danger of torpedo explosions in the hangar deck, the *Hammann* backed clear. The *Hammann*'s whaleboat was again dispatched and finally succeeded in dragging clear the remaining four or five life rafts."

He would extol captain and crew of the plucky *Hammann* for "superb seamanship . . . courage without equal . . . outstanding performance."

"Pat" Dowling was "among the last to leave, not the least worried as there were lots of ships and life rafts close by. Everyone had on life jackets."

Ray Laird, satisfied that there were no more wounded, shinnied down the falls (ropes) from boat davits. Somewhat to his surprise, he was joined on a raft by the captain's steward holding "Wags." The spaniel himself was swathed in a life jacket.

Other survivors could have sworn they had seen the dog swimming. Laird, however, obtained the impression that "Wags" was quite dry.

"I watched the men who leaped into the water," wrote Chaplain Forgy on the *New Orleans*. "Their arms moved as though they were swimming, but they seemed to struggle, unmoving, in the same spot. Little spots of bright yellow began appearing here and there about the burning carrier as men pulled the rubber life rafts from the *Lex*'s planes, threw them into the sea and jumped in after them.

"About fifty of the carrier's proud planes huddled with folded wings like frightened birds at the end of her deck as orange fingers of fire poked through the black smoke and felt about the flat landing area for some place to grab hold.

"Between the *No-Boat* and the *Lex* the sea was dotted with little black bumps that were the heads of struggling sailors. Boats from our cruiser and the destroyers moved back and forth, pulling the men from the water. Distance at sea fools a lot of people. The *No-Boat* seemed but a short city block from the stricken flattop, and many of the *Lexington* men thought they could swim it with no trouble. A couple of them came aboard the cruiser hale and hearty; most of them fell to the deck, half-drowned and exhausted, after being pulled from the sea.

"Lines dangled from the *No-Boat* deck to the water about every ten feet on the port side. Five or six men crowded about the deck at each line.

"Twenty feet off the side of the cruiser a figure splashed almost listlessly in the water. He had swum all the way over from the carrier, but it seemed the energy necessary to propel his tortured body the remaining few feet had been spent. He appeared to be treading water rather than swimming. He pawed at the water intermittently and then just lay there, moving his arms and legs only enough to keep his nose above the surface.

" 'Keep coming, mate, just a little bit more and you'll make it!' shouted one of the sailors at the top of a line near me.

184

"They hauled the line to the deck and tossed it outward toward the struggling man in the water. The swimmer lifted his arms and grabbed at the air, but the line fell short, hung on the surface a couple of seconds, then sank from sight.

"The men on the deck hauled the line back feverishly. One of the raced for a life preserver.

" 'Keep coming, Mac,' the man with the rope encouraged the pitiful figure in the water. 'We'll get you this time.'

"The *No-Boat* men made the life preserver fast to the end of the line and hurled it over the side. It splashed into the water and sent a green-white spray over the bobbing head. I watched the man's hands as they grasped the line. His fists clenched about the rope with the strength of steel vises.

" 'Hey, Mac! Put your leg through that life preserver and hang on,' one of the men called from the deck.

"The swimmer obeyed automatically. Eagerly the men pulled him aboard. They grabbed each side of his dripping body as he came over the side and shook the life preserver from his leg.

"The lad, a short, two-hundred-pound Filipino cook, collapsed to the deck with a soggy thud. His brown, tropical skin seemed to glow a weird bluish color.

" 'He couldn't be that fat,' observed one of the sailors. 'He must be full of water.'

"There was no time to call for corpsmen. One man rolled the portly islander to his stomach. Another pulled out his tongue and adjusted the man's head on his limp arm.

"The water-soaked Filipino was nearly dead. When a husky sailor straddled his back and began artificial respiration, unbelievable volumes of water gushed from his nose and mouth with each stroke.

" 'Keep pushing,' one of the sailors encouraged the man on the Filipino's back. 'That guy's got about half the Coral Sea aboard.'

"The half-drowned figure on the deck grunted and coughed a couple of times. I leaned close to his face and heard him breathe and moan softly.

185

" 'He's going to be all right,' I said to the sailors working on him. 'Good work. Get him in a blanket as soon as you can.'

"As I walked forward to the well deck the scene was being repeated a dozen times. The sailors lining the side of the ship looked like an excursion of fishermen during the mackerel run. They stood there tossing their lines into the water and hauling their catches back to the deck. Artificial respiration was being applied to prone bodies scattered all along the deck.

"Flames, bright orange against the black smoke, were racing aft on the carrier's flight deck now. Only a few men, most of them officers who had been directing the abandonment, remained on the deck. They were clustered in a little group at the bow. They were too far away for me to make out faces or rank insignia, but I knew Captain Sherman of the *Lexington* was among them. He would be the last man to leave the ship.

"The flames worked their way back to the planes bunched together at the stern. One of the planes caught fire, blazed brightly a few seconds as the flames ran through its wings, then exploded. Plumes of burning gasoline shot like rockets into the air and fell upon the other planes. There was another explosion, and then another, as each plane let go with fiery anger. I could hear the sharp crackling of the dry, tinder-like warbirds as the after portion of the *Lexington* became a huge mass of red and yellow.

"The figures at the front of the carrier dived and jumped into the water as fuel tanks from the blazing aircraft sent streams of fire spitting across the deck as though they came from the deadly nozzles of flamethrowers. A boat moved in close to the carrier to pick up the final handful of survivors."

Meanwhile, another chaplain was trying to quit a ship.

"When only half a dozen men were left on the bow," Chaplain Markle wrote, "I suggested to Dr. Roach that he go down a line, and I followed him off the port bow.

"I had trouble swimming away. The swells kept me against the side of the ship and I was tired anyway. That was the only time I really felt frightened.

"Finally I got out from under the overhang of the flight deck and lay on my back taking it easy."

Dr. Roach also found it "very difficult" to stroke away from the derelict, noting: "I tried several times swimming directly away from the side and accomplished nothing. At first I thought it was the old question of suction which we had all heard about, but I found out soon that the ship was drifting down on me about the same rate at which I could swim.

"The total result was that I made no progress. I then discovered I could swim forward along the side. The people who went over the starboard had considerable difficulty there, too. In that case, the wind and the waves continually forced them back toward the ship, so we all found that about the only way we could make any headway was by swimming either forward or aft and getting away from the ship at either the bow or the stern.

"When I approached the bow I found then that I could swim directly away from the ship and proceeded a distance of approximately 150 yards when a boat from the cruiser *Minneapolis* came along and pulled me aboard. Even though the water was warm when I was picked up, I found I was completely exhausted. We had been working hard all day long and had nothing to eat, nothing to drink. That in conjunction with rather vigorous swimming tired me considerably."

Dr. Roach was luckier than some who piled into another whaleboat from the same cruiser. This one, overloaded in a rush, was swamped.

Chaplain Markle, a chunky and powerful man, swam half the distance to the "nearest destroyer." Then he grabbed hold of a raft. He found it was drifting away faster than he could control it by doing a flutter kick.

"Soon a boat came," he continued, "and picked up all of us on that raft. It took us to the *New Orleans* where I climbed up a cargo net."

At six o'clock, "Red" Gill, by now on a rescue destroyer, would log, "*Lex* continuing to blow up."

Seven minutes later, at 1807, the *Morris'* duty officer

watched a "terrific" explosion as flames "spread along the deck and through the planes on deck, shot out of the stack."

Sherman took refuge "under the edge of the flight deck to avoid the falling pieces . . . planes and debris of all kinds went high into the air."

At 1819, sunset, the *Anderson* "darkened ship."

"All the crew were off," it seemed to Sherman. "The water around the ship was black with the bobbing heads of swimmers. Small boats from our escorts, cruisers and destroyers were busy picking men out of the water."

One of them, "Rip" Raring, had waited for quite some time on the fantail with a landing signal officer, smoking cigarettes in an outward show of calm. Then he had lowered himself by rope onto a raft.

With some assistance, Raring propelled the raft away from the carrier by kicking out, even as Markle and others had done. It was much as though he were lying upon a surfboard.

In fact, in the gentle swell of evening, with the skies somewhat clearing, the aerologist experienced a paradoxical sense of well-being. He entertained few worries over sharks since he was certain the "commotion" would scare them off.

"This is cocktail time," he thought, inappropriate as the place and circumstances.

Sherman, at 1830, decided it was time to go, whatever others might have attributed to the moment. After making "a last inspection," he could record, "to insure that there were no stragglers, I stood with Commander Seligman at the stern. I directed him to leave, as it was my duty and privilege to be the last one to go. He went down into the water.

"I stood on the great ship alone. . . .

"Having assured myself there was no other living person aboard, I went down a line hand over hand."

19

"... like the lady she was."

Fred Hartson saw the captain of the *Lexington*, momentarily, on the rope. A cigarette, as always, drooped from his lips. Fred thought this to be quite singular indeed.

Then Sherman, agile old sea dog that he was, as he himself would recall, "dropped off into the water." He was not afloat long. A whaleboat from the *Hammann*, awaiting him —in fact, under orders from Admiral Fitch to prevent any "funny stuff"—picked up the commanding officer and transferred him to another launch from the *Minneapolis*.

On the latter cruiser, Dr. Roach had lost no time in putting on dry clothes and getting to work in the sick bay that had been set up in the captain's quarters.

"We had quite a large number of wounded, some of them seriously," he observed, "most of them of rather minor nature. . . . It was quite a long and protracted job."

There were now 500 survivors on board the *Minneapolis*, the greatest number brought onto any of the rescue fleet, although the plucky little *Hammann* was herself crowded with 478 officers and men. There was literally no place to sit down, on either vessel.

The sick bay on the *New Orleans* was full, too, according to Chaplain Forgy. A temporary ward was set up in the hangar that accommodated the cruiser's four aircraft.

"I made my way through the crowded deck," Forgy wrote. "There were hundreds of men from the *Lexington* jammed aboard the *New Orleans* now, and more were coming. A couple of dozen of them, wrapped in blankets, huddled about a steaming coffee pot. They looked like blanketed Indians powwowing around a campfire.

"I reported to Dr. Farquhar in the hangar. Doc and a corpsman were going down the long rows of the wounded, who were stretched out on the deck. They were spraying paraffin solution from flit-guns upon the burned hands and legs of the *Lexington* men. The paraffin hardened in a few seconds and protected the horrible wounds from infection. I thanked God for the paraffin we had found in that grocery store.

" 'What do you need, Doc?' I inquired.

" 'Blankets, padre. Lots of blankets for these fellows. We've used up all the medical department's supply.'

"With a party of men I ran down to the sleeping compartments below. We grabbed every blanket we could find. There was no time for the formality of requisitions or orders. We just ripped blankets off the cots and hurried them up to the hangar.

"The long rows of wounded extended from the after part of the hangar forward through the hangar and across the well deck to the crew's galley. There were about 150 men lying there on the deck. Many of them were suffering from sheer physical exhaustion and immersion. They were nauseated and shook under terrific chills. They coughed up gallons of seawater to the deck beside them. There were far too few basins.

"Others sat upright and held out their hands with palms upraised. They said nothing, but there was a pleading in their eyes as they waited for corpsmen to come along and spray the soothing paraffin on the seared raw meat left by

190

friction burns when they slid down the lines from their mortally wounded carrier.

"Most of the men in this emergency sick bay were so-called mobile cases. Among them, though, were many seriously wounded men who should have been in the main sick bay below. But there was no room down there.

"I heard a low, continuous moan and moved down the long row of pain to a young Marine gunner. A corpsman working on the boy didn't have to undress him. He merely pulled the shreds of what was left of his uniform away from the lad's charred skin and threw them to the deck. . . ."

Fred Hartson had been in the water nearly an hour and a half and dusk was coming. He was becoming increasingly worried about being picked up when, with seeming abruptness, a motor whaleboat materialized and hauled him out.

"Here's a cigarette," someone offered him before he was scarcely in the boat. It was a Chesterfield. Someone stepped on his stomach as he tried to stretch out in the crowded launch. He didn't seem to care.

On the *Anderson*, Harold Littlefield was given dry clothing, "several cups of hot coffee and a temporary patch on my arm. Shortly after they passed out cigarettes and matches to us, the cooks started going on chow. They turned out a favorite American dish: fried eggs and ham.

"And for a destroyer that is really putting out chow! We never had fried eggs on the *Lex*."

Topsides on the *Anderson,* her duty officer noted at 1840, "One *Anderson* boat crew and *Lexington* personnel aboard picked up by *Dewey*. Boat was abandoned."

One minute later he added, "*Phelps* ordered to sink *Lexington,* using torpedoes."

Aboard the *Phelps*, Beck wrote, "With crew removed to other ships and mine, I received from OTC Fletcher [Officer in Tactical Command,] 'Make one more sweep around and close aboard *Lex* to determine all men removed from ship and water, then sink her with torpedoes and rejoin.'

"Why should this inglorious assignment fall to me? The thought was sickening. Rather that it had been the *Shokaku!*"

191

Aboard the *Phelps* was Ray Laird and also "Wags." Sherman, however, not advised of the safety of his pet, had already started a query bouncing around the ships of the task force: "Who has a cocker spaniel aboard? Repeat . . ."

Ten minutes before 7 o'clock, the *Anderson* recorded: "Second *Anderson* boat crew and *Lexington* personnel aboard picked up by *Dewey*. Boat was abandoned. These two boats were out on rescue work. They were abandoned due to engine breakdowns (line from life raft was fouled in propeller of gig boat), water flooded engine space of motor whaleboat."

Two minutes later, the report said, *"Lexington* burning fiercely fore and aft with many explosions occurring."

On the *Anderson,* following his feast of fried eggs, Littlefield noted "it was almost dark. Off in the distance our old *Lady Lex,* flaming from stem to stern. It was a sad sight, a sort of fury in all its glory . . . we pulled away fast. . . ."

From another destroyer, Noel Gayler was able to discern that the elevator of the *Lexington* "had blown up out of her and was lying on its back on the flight deck. Big chunks were blown off by the various explosions but she was still floating."

At just four minutes before 7, *Anderson* logged, "Proceeded to rejoin *Yorktown*. Set course 200° (T) speed 22 knots."

At 7:02 the destroyer changed course 25 more degrees westward and reduced speed to 14 knots.

Long after the *Lexington* was "over the horizon," Littlefield "could see the fiery glow in the sky."

Aboard the cruiser *Portland,* Robert Griffith, who had been on duty at the carrier's arresting gear, "could see aircraft exploding on the flight deck and the tracer bullets arcing out from the guns . . . she was a solid mass of flame."

From the *New Orleans,* Markle described the carrier as "bright red, glowing like an ember, lighting the whole sky." The chaplain then "went back down." He did not have the heart to see more.

To Captain Sherman, bareheaded on a bridge wing of the *Minneapolis,* "the picture of the burning and doomed ship was a magnificent and awe-inspiring but sad sight . . . lit up by her flames in the gathering darkness."

Lieutenant Swanson, also on the *Minneapolis,* feared the blazing derelict's "brilliant lighting" would act as a beacon to "enemy aircraft." Other officers estimated that the incandescent spectacle might be visible to airplanes flying off the tip of New Guinea, nearly 200 miles to the northwest.

"The fleet departed," Beck continued, "and *Phelps* was left behind to perform her black task. A heavy cloud of smoke rose skyward and we took station to windward.

"One, two, three 'fish' were fired."

The concussion as felt on the *Morris* was "similar to that of depth charges."

Even in the dark, Stanley Johnston, aboard the *Minneapolis,* saw "A vast upheaval of water" on the starboard side of the *Lexington.* "For a moment this appeared to be a Niagara against the flames, then it fell back and the *Lex* was still burning."

As Sherman observed, "the torpedoes hit and exploded with dull booms. The stricken vessel started getting deeper in the water . . . slowly going down, as if she too was reluctant to give up the battle."

For the fulfillment of the *Phelps'* orders, the carrier was sinking much *too* slowly. Ray Laird, watching, had the impression that there was "exploder trouble" with the torpedoes.

Beck, who thought "the Old Lady" still "rode majestically," ordered two more torpedoes from the "opposite quarter."

Dudley, the exhausted navigator asleep aboard the *Hammann,* was awakened by the officer of the deck who asked: "Don't you want to see the last of your ship, sir?"

Dudley yawned, thought, then thanked the watch officer as he replied, "Hell, no."

And he went back to sleep.

Duckworth, aboard the same destroyer, already had sat down to recapitulate the day:

"Upon commencing to write this report . . . I discovered that my mind was filled with a confused group of events which were difficult to arrange in their proper order. The de-

tails of the events were perfectly clear but their arrangement in proper order was impossible. . . ."

The *Lexington,* by her navigator's last position estimate, was going to her death in 2,000 fathoms of water—more than two miles—at latitude 15° 15′ south, longitude 155° 35′ east, or about 200 miles south of Rossel Island.

At 1940 "Red" Gill reported the *Lexington* still afloat and "burning."

The *Phelps'* second salvo hit. In a moment Beck watched "the *Lex* disappear serenely."

To Sherman, from his farther perspective, she went down "with her colors proudly flying and the last signal flags reading, 'I am abandoning ship,' still waving at the yardarm . . . on an even keel, like the lady she always was."

Barely below the surface, however, the "lady" proved not so serene—or even ladylike—as her torpedo warheads finally let go. The *Phelps* was "heaved high out of the water" to come down, painfully, with the clatter of an upended hardware store.

Startled, her communications officer sent off a message, the destroyer's "stern blown off," then as quickly reported this was "in error."

Fourteen miles distant, the *New Orleans* "shook," Markle attested, "as though she had been hit by a torpedo." Other ships twenty miles afar experienced the same shock.

The time was four minutes before 8 P.M., May 8, 1942, far out in the Coral Sea. And it was night again, as if giant floodlights had winked out.

Captain Sherman, still spellbound, pronounced his own amen: "It was the end of the *Lexington.*"

Or *was* it?

Would there be more *Lexingtons* for winning a war that had started in earnest, and with the presentiment of victory?

Whether or not the carrier could really die in the hearts of all who had known and served upon her and loved her, right now she was gone. And those, such as Hank Laupan, the accordion player, watching from across the night waters, just "wanted to bawl like babies."

196

Postscript

Captain Sherman reported to the Navy Department that he had lost 26 officers and 190 men out of the complement of 2,951.

"This in itself," he asserted, "is considered to be a remarkable record. The ship and crew had performed gloriously and it seemed too bad that she had to perish in her hour of victory. But she went to a glorious end, more fitting than the usual fate of the eventual scrap heap or succumbing to the perils of the sea."

The next month he could spell out that the *Lexington* by her sacrifice had deprived the enemy of two carriers at Midway—two carriers that in all likelihood made the slim difference between victory and defeat.

As the historian, Samuel Eliot Morison, would observe:

"Call Coral Sea what you will, it was an indispensable preliminary to the great victory at Midway . . . that story of the last fight of *'Lady Lex,'* her calm abandonment, the devotion of her crew to their ship and their captain transcend mere history. The American people took it to their hearts and stored it up in the treasury of folk memory."

Japanese artist Nakamura Ken-Ichi's painting "Sea Battle of the Coral Sea" recalls the fury of those crucial days in May, 1942.

The long road back from Pearl Harbor which started in earnest with the Coral Sea ended in Tokyo Bay with complete victory.

Erich Eger

Tom Nixon

Some
who
remember:

Len Olliff

John S. Wood

Adm. Herbert S. Duckworth

U.S.S. *Lexington*
REPORT of CASUALTIES

(This is the verbatim casualty report as filed by the executive officer from Tonga Tabu atoll.)

1. The following officers were killed in action on May 8, 1942, except as noted:

NAME	RANK
BARRY, M.F.	Electrician, U.S.N.
GILMORE, W.W.	Commander, (SC), U.S.N.
HEALY, H.R.	Lieut. Comdr., U.S.N.
JOHNS, P.H.	Ensign, U.S.N.R.
PRICE, E.M.	Lieut (jg), U.S.N.
TROJAKOWSKI, W.C.	Commander, (DC), U.S.N.
WHITHAM, J.E.	Gunner, U.S.N.
ZIEHR, C.H.	Ensign, U.S.N.
ZWIERSCHKE, R.H.	Ensign, (SC), U.S.N.R.

2. The following officers are missing since May 8, 1942, except as noted:

AULT, W.B.	Command, U.S.N.	CLAG
ALLEN, E.H. [a]	Lieutenant, U.S.N.	VS-2
BAKER, P.G. [a]	Lieut (jg), U.S.N.	VF-2
BULL, R.S., JR.	Lieutenant, U.S.N.	VF-2
CLARK, H.F.	Lieut (jg), U.S.N.	VF-3
HALE, R.O., JR.	Lieut (jg), U.S.N.	VS-2
MASON, N.H.	Ensign, U.S.N.R.	VF-3
PETERSON, D.W.	Ensign, U.S.N.R	VF-3
QUIGLEY, A.J. [a b]	Ensign, U.S.N.R	VS-2
ROWELL, R.M.	Ensign, U.S.N.R.	VF-3
RINEHART, C.F.	Lieut (jg), U.S.N.	VF-2
THORNHILL, L.W.	Lieut (jg), U.S.N.	VT-2
WINGFIELD, J.D.	Ensign, U.S.N.R.	VS-2
WOOD, H. [b]	Ensign, U.S.N.R	VS-2

---

[a] — Missing since May 7, 1942.
[b] — Reported Rescued.

1. The following men were killed in action on May 8, 1942, except as noted:

NAME	SERVICE NO.	RATE
ALTO, Eino J.	328 46 27	EM1c
ARCHIBALD, Edmund W.	368 68 88	Sea2c
BLINCOE, Michael, V.	382 55 37	Sea2c
BOHLANDER, Frank W., Jr.	356 63 55	Sea2c
BOHNER, Theodore R.	376 31 07	Sea2c
BROWN, Eddie L. Jr.	272 25 06	SC3c
BROWN, Robert Van B.	342 17 06	SK3c
BULT, Thomas K.	368 25 62	QM1c
CARLSON, Albert E.	311 42 21	CM3c
CARLSON, John B.	316 47 44	SK2c
COLEMAN, Donald E.	342 43 83	Sea2c
DAVIS, Jess O.	320 72 03	MM1c
DIAMOND, Theodore L.	337 33 55	Sea2c
DULL, Burl W.	300 11 79	CM3c
DUNN, John J.	266 19 97	F3c
DUPREE, William J.	360 34 76	F3c
DURANT, Howard E., Jr.	413 55 43	Sea2c
EDWARDS, Kenneth O.	337 40 18	SF3c
ELY, Robert C.	385 83 33	Sea1c
FLATT, Garfield H.	368 42 72	MM2c
FORTNER, Roscoe L.	287 45 55	SK3c
FRASURE, Hershell D.	287 53 40	Sea2c
FURMAN, Burton J.	680 00 40	SK3c
GARREN, "J" "B"	295 74 05	F1c
GIBBS, Nathaniel	262 95 92	Matt3c
GOULD, Howard S.	662 06 35	SK3c
HALL, Elby L.	346 76 80	MM2c
HART, Thomas H.	268 79 12	Sea2c
HENRY, Joel Q.	295 74 16	Sea2c
HOFSTRA, George J.	382 44 20	Sea2c
HOWARD, James E.	346 83 43	SK3c
JAQUES, Ray L	337 48 14	Y3c
JEMISON, Eugene	272 71 37	Matt2c

202

NAME	SERVICE NO.	RATE
JOHNSON, Ralph E.	272 38 49	SC3c
JONES, Edgar	342 39 20	AMM3c
KANE, William J.	414 41 42	SK3c
KIDD, James W.	291 60 78	SC3c
KING, John M.	356 92 13	EM1c
KING, Kenneth R.	356 63 36	Sea2c
KRAUSE, John H.	404 93 66	F1c
LETTOW, Charles A.	321 37 85	Cox
LEWANDOWSKI, Arthur A.	328 60 06	M1dr2c
LIBBY, Robert L.	223 45 24	SF2c
LITTLE, James L.	295 32 75	SF2c
LOCKARD, Joseph R.	382 48 98	Sea2c
LYNN, Estus L.	337 07 97	SF3c
MACDOUGALL, Eugene R.	299 99 90	Y2c
MARTIN, Earl W.	300 19 74	SK3c
McLAIN, Robert M.	393 05 38	CEM(AA)
MENDIOLA, Francisco N.	421 07 50	Matt2c
MILLER, Richard C.	616 02 32	Y3c
MILLER, Stephen J.	299 77 57	SF2c
NOFTSGER, Ernest H.	342 00 93	GM2c
NUNES, William W.	662 04 63	Sea2c
O'DELL, Charles H.	316 78 35	Sea2c
O'NEAL, Willie (n)	346 73 87	Matt1c
OHLER, William G.	375 55 75	CEM(AA)
ORR, Manley S.	262 46 81	EM3c
PAGE, Warren W.	393 49 15	Sea1c
PENNYBACKER, Frank H.	295 75 41	SF3c
RAMSDEN, Marvin L.	389 97 04	Cox
RASBERRY, Mahlon E.	360 43 46	Sea2c
ROSE, Joseph E.	311 39 44	GM3c
RUPERT, Dale E.	368 58 56	SF3c
RELERFORD, Nathaneail L.	346 83 52	Matt2c
SCHAMP, Delbert D. [a]	316 75 20	Sea2c
SCHNEIDER, Albert J.	360 07 92	F1c
SMITH, Carlyle G.	238 69 32	Ptr3c

[a] — Died of wounds 5-15-42

NAME	SERVICE NO.	RATE
SMITH, Vernon C.	372 15 51	EM3c
SNYDER, Glenn L.	337 04 10	Sea1c
STASKO, John, Jr.	238 69 05	SF3c
STRAUS, David "H", Jr.	624 03 42	SK2c
THAU, Willard A.	375 78 49	MM1c
VASS, Frank I., Jr.	382 29 28	Sea2c
WHITE, Eugene A.	266 39 14	Sea2c
WHITE, Lester J.	381 21 53	GM3c
WHITELEY, Robert L.	372 19 82	Bkr3c
WILKERSON, Claude M.	360 18 78	SK3c
WILLIAMS, Alter L.	287 31 13	Matt1c
WILLSON, Charles E.	201 78 18	SC3c
YOUNG, Carl C.	295 75 37	Sea1c
ZEIGLER, Harry D.	243 77 14	Y3c
ZILINEK, Victor J.	223 87 70	GM3c

COM CAR DIV ONE

PARKER, Richard E.	632 10 66	Matt3c

SCOUTING SQUADRON TWO

BUTLER, William T. [b]	223 24 91	ARM1c
DAVIS, William P. [b]	283 93 69	AOM3c
EDWARDS, John O.	212 52 95	ARM2c
HUVAR, Cyril F., Jr. [c]	360 27 79	RM3c
LACKEY, John D. [b]	316 61 47	ARM2c
ROUSER, Charles W., Jr. [b]	328 69 41	ARM2c
WHEELHOUSE, Robert E. [c]	300 07 93	ARM3c

[b] — Missing since 5-8-42.

[c] — Reported rescued from Rossel Island.

FIGHTING SQUADRON TWO

HOLCOMB, Allen D.	386 03 75	Sea2c
WEEKS, Virgil L.	265 85 24	PhM2c
HUDSON, Norman, Jr.	279 — —	OC3c

TORPEDO SQUADRON TWO

GLOVER, Wilmer T. [b]	262 27 70	AOM2c
HELDOORN, Johannas C. [b]	401 36 53	AMM1c

[b] — Missing since 5-8-42.

Acknowledgments

The author wishes to thank especially for their generous and continuing aid these survivors of the *Lexington*: Vice Admiral Herbert S. Duckworth, USN (ret.), Jacksonville, Florida; Rear Admiral James R. Dudley, USN (ret.), Leesburg, Virginia; Erich Eger, Pewaukee, Wisconsin; Lieutenant Thomas Jones Nixon III, USN (ret.), Wilson, North Carolina; Rear Admiral E. J. O'Donnell, USN (ret.), President, Maritime College, State University of New York, the Bronx, New York; Captain George Raring, USN (ret.), Santa Fe, New Mexico. All of these officers also aided in checking the manuscript for technical accuracy.

The author also acknowledges the splendid assistance of: Donald Albrightson, Sunnyvale, California; Captain Evan P. Aurand, USN, Fairfax, Virginia (not aboard at the time of the sinking); Rear Admiral E. L. Beck, USN (ret.), Bradenton, Florida; Frank Binder, Jacksonville, Florida; Vice Admiral Elliott Buckmaster, USN (ret.), Coronado, California; Conley Cain, Jacksonville, Florida; Captain Asbury Coward,

USN (ret.), Falls Church, Virginia; Commander Cecil E. Dowling, USN (ret.), Lomita, California; Admiral Aubrey W. Fitch, USN (ret.), Newcastle, Maine; Chaplain Howell M. Forgy, USN (ret.), Glendora, California; David Fox and Edward Fox, Wawatosa, Wisconsin; Captain R. C. Gillette, USN, Bethesda, Maryland (not aboard); Vice Admiral Noel Gayler, USN, Offutt Air Force Base, Nebraska; Robert E. Griffith, San Diego, California; Fred T. Hartson, Portsmouth, New Hampshire; Captain G. Roy Hartwig, USN (ret.), Potomac, Maryland; Vernon W. Highfill, Ventura, California; Rear Admiral Gilbert C. Hoover, USN (ret.), Bristol, Rhode Island; Vice Admiral Harry B. Jarrett, USN (ret.), Washington, D.C.; Lester Jones, Jacksonville, Florida; Captain W. R. Laird Jr., USN (ret.), Sioux Falls, South Dakota; James V. Landis, Pensacola, Florida; Henry Laupan, Franklin, Wisconsin; Harold R. Littlefield, Santa Rosa, California; Captain Hoyt D. Mann, USN (ret.), Coronado, California; Chaplain George Markle, USN (ret.), Carmel, California; Frank M. McKenzie, Baltimore, Maryland; Captain Edward Muhlenfeld, USN, Falls Church, Virginia; Commander Jesse L. Near, USN (ret.), Boulder, Colorado (not aboard); L. L. Olliff, Warrington, Florida; Mrs. Frederick C. Sherman, San Diego, California; Captain Chandler Swanson, USN (ret.), Winter Park, Florida; Rear Admiral Arnold True, USN (ret.), La Honda, California; Captain Mark T. Whittier, USN (ret.), Monterey, California (not aboard); Commander Harold E. Williamson, USN (ret.), Camarillo, California; John Wood, Haines City, Florida.

The author wishes to pay respect to the memory of these officers who left behind graphic records of those last hours in the Coral Sea: Lieutenant F. F. Gill; Rear Admiral Alexander F. Junker; Captain Morton T. Seligman, Admiral Frederick Carl Sherman and Dr. Arthur J. White.

Other testimony provided immediately after the sinking which proved helpful was from Lieutenant W. B. Durant, the assistant supply officer, Dr. J. F. Roach and Lieutenant

Charles Williams, another assistant supply officer, whose whereabouts are unknown.

A great many others not necessarily connected with the *Lexington* or the Battle of the Coral Sea also helped make possible this book, including James W. Cheevers, Curator, U.S. Naval Academy Museum; Admiral E. M. Eller, Director, Naval History, Dean Allard and others associated with him; S. A. Gabaldon and Lieutenant Commander Walter Reed, of the Minutemen, an association of shipmates who had served on the *Lex* at one time or another, both of whom aided materially in locating survivors. Nor should the author's wife, Mary, and daughter, Clara, be overlooked, since they accompanied him on much of the travel essential to this research.

Public Affairs staffs at the Pensacola and Jacksonville Naval Air Stations also provided direct assistance in the research.

Books, periodicals and newspapers were of secondary import since this book is based for the most part on interviews, correspondence, official reports and other prime research. However, Stanley Johnston's own account was contained in the book, *Queen of the Flattops,* published by E. P. Dutton and Co. (New York) in 1942, shortly after the event. Sherman published his memoirs of the war years, *Combat Command,* (also Dutton) in 1950, while his wife, Fanny Jessop Sherman, immortalized the captain's spaniel in *Admiral Wags,* for young people, published in 1943 (Dodd, Mead, New York). Chaplain Forgy wrote his story, . . . *and Pass the Ammunition* (Appleton-Century Co., New York) in 1944, from which most of his quotations are taken since, as is also the case with Chaplain Markle, the Reverend Forgy has been in ill health.

Part of Littlefield's reminiscences was contained in the October, 1942 "QST," publication of the American Radio Relay League. Samuel Eliot Morison's quote on the Coral Sea is from his *History of United States Naval Operations in World War II,* Vol. 4, "Coral Sea, Midway and Submarine Actions," Little Brown and Company, Boston, 1947–1962.

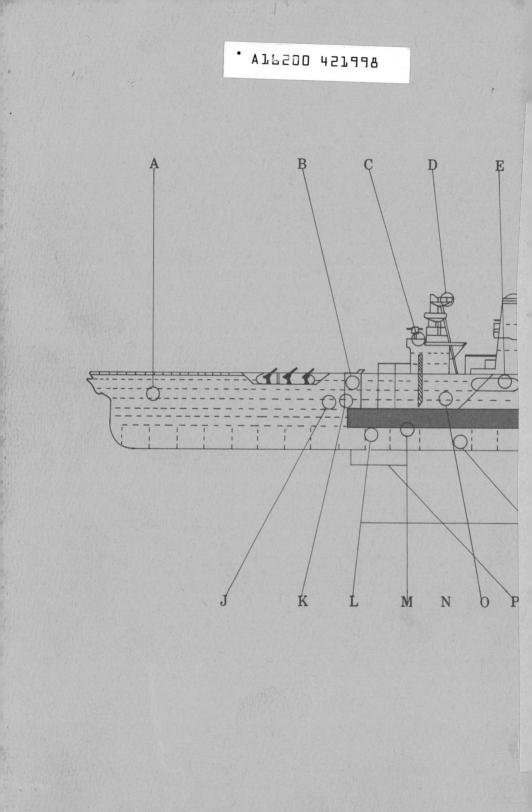